CONTENTS

Foreword: BIM for Estates

Chapter 1: Introduction 7

Chapter 2: BIM: The container for your building data 13

Chapter 3: A data-centric culture 33

Chapter 4: Establishing your organisational
data requirements 51

Chapter 6: Model checking 83

Chapter 7: BIM competency 101

Chapter 8: Classifications 117

Chapter 9: Risk 145

Chapter 10: Data maintenance 157

Chapter 11: Employer's Information Requirements (EIR) 173

Chapter 12: Organisational and Asset Information
Requirements (OIR and AIR) 223

Chapter 13 - Employer's data requirements
and BIM data template 231

Chapter 14: Final comments 249

Chapter 15 - Glossary of terms 255

BIM FOR ESTATES: ABOUT THE AUTHOR

Ian Yeo, a chartered civil engineer (CEng) and business person of the year (Hull and East Yorkshire Chamber of Commerce), has more than 20 years' experience within the construction industry. For the majority of this time, Ian has been involved in design management of education and health projects, working for national and local contractors.

In 2016, after a period of five years of learning and implementing BIM at Sewell Construction, Ian and his co-founder Scott Pilgrim started BIMsense. BIMsense focuses on bringing the benefits of BIM to large estate clients. BIMsense has since received recognition for its approach including digital business of the year (Yorkshire and Humberside Federation of Small Businesses).

Ian fuses a passion for BIM innovation and continuous improvement with a background in design management, civil engineering, and project development and delivery. This enables Ian and his team to provide large estate clients and their wider project teams with uniquely experienced support.

FOREWORD: BIM FOR ESTATES

As a former vice-chancellor of universities, an advocate of BIM and indeed all technology that improves systems, processes and life in general, Professor Calie Pistorius, CEO of DeltaHedron Ltd, and former Vice-Chancellor of the University of Pretoria and the University of Hull was the natural choice for us to approach to write our foreword.

Having experienced the challenges that large estates teams are tasked with in terms of the ongoing development of new facilities, and the extension, refurbishment and renovation of existing spaces, Calie understands the impact BIM has in providing a collaborative platform in which to design, construct and maintain built assets.

Space utilisation, energy efficiencies and programme risk reduction are all key to the development of further education estates, and indeed any estate. Suffice to say, BIM is now being seen as the way forward in successfully achieving the objectives within these areas.

It is our absolute pleasure that Calie agreed to review our book and present this foreword.

The construction industry is one of great strategic importance on regional, national and global levels. Economic growth, quality of life, competitiveness and security all depend on new infrastructure and the maintenance of older structures.

The construction industry has been dogged by many concerns for some decades. The industry is indeed not just ripe for change, but is poised for drastic disruption. A range of emerging technologies are collectively driving change and will be catalysts for disruption. Robotics, 3D printing, modular construction, automation and other advances in manufacturing, drones, wearables and new construction materials will all have a transformative impact on the industry and contribute to a wave of creative destruction in construction.

Digitisation of the construction industry is certainly one of the most powerful and prominent forces that will accelerate the disruption of construction. Digital transformation is one of the most significant global trends. It impacts every sector of society, driving progress, economic growth and quality of life.

No industry is left untouched or immune. Mindful that there is a direct correlation between the extent to which an industry is digitised and productivity growth, it is not surprising to note that construction is one of the least digitised industries. This is bound to change.

Digital-related technologies such as mobile and cloud-based applications will underpin a number of other emerging digital and data technologies. These will in turn enhance the quality of data-driven decision-making and productivity. As part of the digitisation process, the construction industry will increasingly adopt practices which are common cause in other industries, such as software-as-a-service (SaaS), Enterprise Resource Planning (ERP) and bring-your-own-device (BYOD). Emerging data technologies such as big data, analytics, machine learning and artificial intelligence (AI) all have application in the construction industry, and will multiply the impact of digital transformation as they have done in other industries; as will virtual reality (VR) and augmented reality (AR), the Internet of Things (IoT), geolocation and blockchain.

Building Information Modelling (BIM) is a digital technology designed for the construction and estates industries. It brings a new level of machine intelligence, integration and cooperation with consummate gains in effectiveness, efficiency, productivity and competitiveness. BIM can enhance all phases of the process, from the conceptual phase through the iterations of design, tendering and construction. A major component of BIM's value, however, is its application after the building has been completed – a period which far exceeds the construction itself. As the building's digital twin, BIM not only contains all the design information but also archives the building's history of construction, use and maintenance. This information is invaluable with regard to the development of a maintenance strategy, maintaining a healthy and safe environment and the optimisation of energy, environmental and waste efficiencies. The digital timeline embedded in BIM is invaluable for the management of the estates, and hugely beneficial when refurbishment, changes or demolition is required. BIM is a living document for the owners, operators and occupants.

Smart buildings, infrastructure and estates of the future will be intelligent and engage actively and proactively in and with their environment, including the weather, humans, animals and plants. They will have the ability to sense the status of and changes in their environment, make decisions, intervene and respond, and communicate with people, other buildings and devices; and increasingly anticipate, learn and adapt their behaviour. The design of smart buildings needs to be future-proofed. BIM is ideally suited for this task — it is almost inconceivable to think of a construction future without BIM.

The disruption of an industry brings huge opportunities for those who seize them. This is true for the construction industry as well. A number of progressive companies in the industry are already riding the next wave. They have digitised and are adopting innovative business practices and emerging technologies. At the same time, neglect of the impact of the emerging technologies also present risks and threats for the laggards who fumble the future. This is not a time for companies in the construction industry, governments, or those who are considering entering the industry, to be complacent.

It is key is for the construction industry as well as for individual companies, to embrace innovation in its broadest sense. The adoption of BIM - whether on a national level as is already the case in the UK, Singapore and Finland; in the industry; or by individual owners, designers and construction companies - is a leading indicator of the new innovative spirit in the industry. It is the smart thing to do.

There are some encouraging signs, with innovative companies in the industry leading the charge. *BIM for Estates* is timely and addresses the issues from the viewpoint of someone who has dealt with them. The text explains not only the importance of *BIM for Estates* but also provides useful practical guidance.

As the co-founder of BIMsense, an innovative and award-winning constructech company specialising in the development of BIM infrastructure, Ian Yeo has significant experience in this emerging field and is contributing towards the shaping of BIM. The book will be particularly useful for the managers of the estates of educational institutions, but as the author points out, the concepts and principles are applicable to construction projects and estates management across the board. BIM for Estates is highly recommended.

Professor Calie Pistorius, CEng PhD FIET FRSSAf FSAAE FSAIEE
CEO DeltaHedron Ltd, and former Vice-Chancellor of the University of Pretoria and the University of Hull.

CHAPTER 1: INTRODUCTION

DIGITAL TRANSFORMATION

Established industries are changing beyond all recognition.

Digital transformation changes the way that we store, manipulate and communicate the information around us. Information has always existed and it has been subject to continual transformation due to new inventions and evolving technologies. Each new information technology, from the printing press, to the fax, to the personal computer and the internet has spawned new and ingenious methods of using information.

The construction of new buildings requires large amounts of information. From the details of how the building should fit together, the materials to be used, the people and organisations involved in a project, the manuals of how the building works and when everything should happen, all the way through to the details of the actual construction.

Monitoring, controlling and guiding a construction project while understanding all the available information requires a special sort of person, with dedication and skill. But, expecting individuals to be able to access, disseminate and fully understand the implications of such large amounts of information is a risky approach.

Digital transformation of design and construction through the use of Building Information Modelling (BIM), moves project information from being diverse and isolated to being coordinated, centralised and accessible. The information becomes connected, a change to an internal wall instantly changes the data and the effects of that change can be easily understood.

The physical components of a building will always be physical components, but the way that we store, understand and manipulate the information that is required to deliver a facility will continue to change, BIM is just another change, albeit a change that will provide massive benefits.

Facilities are managed and maintained in the most effective way they can be with the information available. Currently, information isn't intentionally withheld from users and maintenance teams, it just isn't provided in a useful and accessible way. If relevant information is provided and made accessible, then better, more informed decisions will be made.

BIM LEVEL 2

The UK government had a large part to play in driving BIM forward. Its BIM mandate required all centrally procured government projects are delivered to a minimum Level 2 BIM maturity from April 2016, providing a push for a lot of organisations to implement the requirements.

The BIM Level 2 guidance documents gave us structure, it required projects to have an Employer's Information Requirements (EIR), the details of a clients BIM deliverables and a BIM Execution Plan (BEP), a statement of how the BIM requirements will be delivered. It also gave us a common vocabulary. The new tools that BIM offered required new words, although many of these new words are acronyms and there are plenty of acronyms in the world of BIM. The new words enabled us to communicate effectively, we understood what was required when someone requested a MPDT (that's a Model Production and Delivery Table).

The BIM Level 2 guidance consisted of a largely untested set of procedures and guidance announced in 2012 and released in 2013, developed by a large team of experts, using the best information available at that time.

As an industry, we have now had the opportunity to test and implement the requirements of BIM Level 2 through thousands of projects. This has given us a greater understanding of what works and where improvements are required.

BIM FOR ESTATES

This book - *BIM for Estates* - is directly written for those who have responsibilities for delivering new building projects for organisations with an estate. The information provided here will also be useful to a wider audience.

An organisation with an estate has arguably the most to be gained from BIM. There are gains through design and construction, with the largest gains being obtained during the use of the facility.

A university or a hospital is a typical organisation with an estate. But, it extends much further to include schools in a multi-academy trust, government departments, commercial organisations, hotels and industrial complexes.

For consistency, the references within this book are primarily focused on education estates. However, the principles can be transferred to any estate organisation.

Throughout this book I also use the terms building and facility. Both terms refer to any built asset within an estate.

THE EVOLUTION OF *BIM FOR ESTATES*

I have lived and breathed BIM for four years before developing the content of this book, debating and questioning with anyone who will listen to me. I have learnt many lessons, tried many different ways of requesting, obtaining and organising model data. I have had to understand the needs of estate's clients and tease out the art of the possible from everyone involved in developing project model. All of which has provided me with practical examples of how BIM can provide enormous benefits for any organisation with a large estate.

This isn't intended to be a technical guide. It's intentionally conversational, to align with the way that the content has been developed. There is a wealth of useful information surrounding BIM. However, despite the increasing volume of BIM guidance and supporting information, I hear all too often, that there remains a lack of clarity among our clients at BIMsense.

I hope to simplify and clarify as much as possible and to put the technical requirements into context. I aim to explain why data and model data is useful, how model data is organised and what you need to put in place to maximise your chances of getting the right information.

For the last two years I have worked closely on BIM projects for large estates clients and before that led the implementation of BIM at a regional contractor. I wouldn't ever claim to know all there is to know about BIM, I wouldn't even claim that I know everything about BIM that is relevant for a large estate. But, I'm sure that what I do know can be useful, and the best way to spread the information to the widest audience possible is through this book.

This book has evolved from one of the regular procedures at BIMsense. Each week, I take an hour to talk through a specific area of BIM. If I'm able to clearly explain the chosen area of BIM then I'm probably close to ensuring that I have a base level of understanding and knowledge. However, our conversations usually result in many queries and questions. These need answering or explaining in various different ways. Each conversation is recorded and converted into text for our records. This became a useful resource, which I wanted to share to a wider audience.

THE STRUCTURE OF THIS BOOK

This book has been arranged so that each chapter introduces new concepts and new ideas. The final chapters provide the most detail and the most complex ideas.

We start the book in *Chapter 2: BIM: The container for your building data* by introducing a different way of looking at digital building models, thinking of them as containers for holding data, nested containers holding increasingly detailed information. Then we move on to some examples of how the data can be used.

We then move into *Chapter 3: A data-centric culture*, which explains why data and information is important and introduces strategies to change your organisational culture to put data at its centre.

Chapter 4: Establishing your organisational data requirements sets out uses for data and specific reasons for collecting data and *Chapter 5: Digital design brief*, brings in the idea that your design brief can be developed in a data format.

Model checking is explored in *Chapter 6: Model checking*, including the reason for model checking and the different types of model checks. With *Chapter 7: BIM competency* providing an overview of BIM competency within your supply chain and the key requirements.

Chapter 8: Classifications explains why a fully classified model is essential to obtain the data benefits of BIM. And Chapter 9: Risk details how your model can be used for managing risks, including project risks and health and safety risks.

Once you have your data within a model it needs maintaining. Chapter 10: Data maintenance explains why this is required and who should maintain your data.

Chapter 11: Employer's information requirements (EIR) provides the detail of what should be contained within an Employer's Information Requirement (EIR) and why it is a key requirement for any BIM project. We then look at the higher-level Organisational Information Requirements and the Asset Information Requirements and how these link back to the EIR in Chapter 12: Organisational and asset information requirements (OIR and AIR).

Finally, *Chapter 13: Employer's data requirements and BIM data template* explains how a data requirements template can provide clear and objective details of the data that you want. Here, you will also find information on how to develop your own data template.

So to summarise, within this book I take a look at the importance of data for an organisation, how BIM can be used for your data, how to establish you data requirements, validating and managing your models, and the tools and methods for establishing your data requirements.

CHAPTER 2: BIM: THE CONTAINER FOR YOUR BUILDING DATA

Container (in computer science) - a data structure whose instances are collections of other objects... they store objects in an organised way. (Wikipedia)

A BIM model provides a visual representation of your estates facility. It aligns the designed visual element of your project with the built physical reality.

In this early chapter I want you to consider your building model in a way that is different from the norm. I want you to consider how your building model is used for storing data. This way of thinking provides a useful metaphor for the rest of this book.

Data can be added to any of the objects within your building model. Each building model has its own data, but each building is also a master data container - it contains spaces that each have their own data. Each space contains objects and each object has data. So, we have data containers within data containers.

Your model provides a visual representation of the rooms within your facility and other elements within those rooms, such as ventilation ducts or boilers.

All these visual elements of your model can be used as containers for storing data. The whole facility - floors, common spaces, zones made up of a group of common spaces and individual components and assets - can be used for storing data.

Some data will only apply to your facility as a whole and only needs to be linked to the master data container. This could be information from the design and construction phase, site investigations or planning consents and it will usually consist of pdf documents. Information for the whole-facility master data container can be easily added to these pdfs - as hyperlinks - when cloud storage is used.

Each individual building component becomes its own data container for specific and detailed data. For example, building components such as an air-handling unit, a fire damper or a door can contain: the name of the manufacturer; a serial number; a warranty start date; a warranty duration; and countless other data attributes.

This provides the asset owner or estate manager with all the information they need to maintain the building efficiently and effectively.

The data that you can add to your facility has no technical limitations. Information can be provided to enable life-cycle costing, operational cost forecasting, tracking compliance, progress during design, and data that enables the assessment and tracking of Building Research Establishment Environmental Assessment Method (BREEAM) sustainability credits. External dynamic data sources can also be linked to the model. Some of these can be generated from the Internet of Things (IoT), through which connected online devices can provide information such as facility usage and people's movements via movement sensors. Dynamic data sources allow your model to become a visual method for analysing and monitoring dynamic information.

PLANNING YOUR BIM DATA MODEL

There is a wide range of possible data uses and options for a facility. It's important to assess and understand your specific needs. We refer to these needs later in Chapter 4 as your employer purposes. These are the ways you intend to use the data, such as using data to schedule your planned preventative maintenance.

Establishing your employer purposes provides a framework for assessing your detailed data requirements. The specific items of data you collect will enable you to meet your employer purposes. But this requires careful management, as the quantity of data collected for one facility can become large very quickly.

Data is added to the project model as the design develops. At the start of a project, the data within the model will be limited. But, the amount of data increases rapidly as a project progresses through the design and construction stages. We take a look at a project's stages in the Chapter 11: Employer's Information Requirements (EIR). Throughout this book, all references to project stages are taken from the RIBA plan of works, which has stages from 0 to 7. These stages take a project from concept (stage 0), through design (stages 1-4), construction (stages 5-6) and use of the facility (stage 7).

Starting your data development at the earliest stages of a project provides an essential structure for the data at all subsequent stages.

> *I cannot stress enough how important it is to ensure that your data is developed in a rational and structured way from the start of a project and then through each subsequent stage.*

The development of data within one stage provides the structure for the data in the next stage. As a project progresses, the quantity of data and the sources of data increase exponentially. Obtaining data at the end of a project without having a data structure in place would be a very difficult process to manage, which is why you need to plan for BIM from the very start.

Almost all project stakeholders will be responsible for adding or providing data for your project model. The number of organisations involved in a project increases at every step of the project, from stage 0 to stage 5 which directly increases the volume of model data:

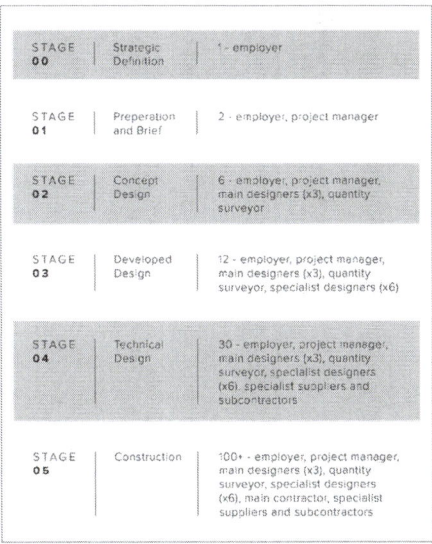

Designers are generally very conscientious and want to enable you to deliver an amazing project. However, if they are not provided with clear guidance they will deliver what they believe you want. I'm not yet aware of any designers who have developed the ability to read minds. And without the ability to read your mind they will not deliver exactly want you want. It could be a reasonable guess, but it will not be exactly what you want. Your project EIR provides your designers with the guidance and framework to ensure they are always working to deliver your specific and exact requirements. This applies to both the finished facility and the data model of the facility.

Adding a robust and comprehensive classification system will make accessing your data considerably easier. A classification system will also enable you to implement future data uses in a simplified way.

A classification system attempts to put all the individual parts of your facility into pre-arranged groups. Standardising these groups across all your projects will make it easier for you to compare projects and extract groupings of data.

Uniclass 2015 (sometimes referred to as is Uniclass2) is a particularly good classification system. We have a whole chapter later in the book on classifications (Chapter 8).

Another important point is that external data links may not remain valid over time.

It was recently considered good practice to provide external links to manufacturers' data. The Construction Operations Building information exchange (COBie) - described by the NBS as "a non-proprietary data format for the publication of a subset of building information models focused on delivering asset data as distinct from geometric information" - was sometimes developed with hyperlinks to manufacturers' literature. The literature would be hosted on a manufacturer's website, as a web page or a link to a downloadable document. The problem is that each link depends upon the manufacturer's website. Generally, websites get updated, revised and web pages change. Links then become invalid or broken. Updating the links provided within COBie then adds an additional layer of administration.

A better approach is to link documentation or specific information to a location within the control of an employer or an estates team. This could be an internal drive location, cloud storage or, ideally, your Common Data Environment, or CDE - a digital place in which project information is stored and shared, such as Asite and Viewpoint. Maintenance of the links will still be required. If the names of drives of folders are altered or changed around, links could still break but, crucially, you will be in control of the changes, you will understand the implications and you will know when changes occur. This highlights the importance of the ever-popular role of the information manager, which we look at in Chapter 7, to validate and maintain your information and the environments in which it is stored.

COLLABORATION

Collaboration is often quoted as being a major benefit of a BIM project and collaboration between project stakeholders does provide significant benefits to a project. Having the latest information available through the project CDE and understanding how the information can be used means everyone can be fully informed.

A BIM project isn't possible without collaboration. Although this doesn't just apply to BIM projects. Any successful construction project with multiple stakeholders will require collaboration.

Collaboration shouldn't be limited to your main designers and shouldn't be limited to ensuring that physical model components fit correctly together. If your project requires an energy analysis, then your model should contain building envelope thermal performance data to enable the project models to be used in the analysis rather than inefficiently developing a separate - and uncoordinated - thermal model. If certain spaces, such as performance spaces and sports halls, require acoustic analysis, then the project models should be developed to contain the acoustic properties of the surface coverings.

These requirements may not be known at the start of the project. But, by reviewing the project requirements with your team you should ensure that your project models remain as the container for your project data.

DATA DEVELOPMENT

Earlier in this chapter we took a look at the organisations involved in a project and how they increase as a project progresses from stage 2 through to stage 5. The number of organisations involved in a project has a direct link to the amount of information generated. Let's now consider how the data itself increases and the types of information that you can expect at each stage.

The data developed during Stage 2 (Concept Design) will be very limited. The facility should be fully defined, it will have a name, a code and an address. Each space within the facility should be defined, with a name, a number and a classification. Each space could also have design brief information, such as occupancy numbers and environmental parameters. There may also be some limited objects within the model, such as doors and windows. These will have basic data to define the objects. But, that could well be the extent of the data within the model. The information will also be provided by one or two designers. It's often normal to only have a single design model at Stage 2, the architectural model.

At Stage 3 (Developed Design), models will be provided by all the main designers, as well as architectural, structural and building services. By Stage 3, the number of designers providing model data has more than doubled from the single designer providing data at Stage 2. This trend continues at each stage continues throughout the project until completion of the facility at Stage 5 (Construction).

I emphasised earlier the importance of a project EIR, it contains the plan for your data. Your plan should be in place from the very earliest stages of any project and definitely before your first designer is appointed. You can use your EIR as part of the appointment process in order to ensure your expectations as the client are set as early as possible. The detail of a project EIR are detailed later in this book, in Chapter 11: Employer's Information Requirements (EIR).

Taking the way data develops as a project progresses as a specific example, an air-handling unit (AHU), may be included in a building services model at Stage 2. At Stage 2, the data would only consist of the name of the AHU and classifications, such as a product and system code. During Stage 3, data would be added to identify the performance requirements of the unit. The performance data enables the specific product data to be developed and added at Stage 4 (Technical Design), such as a manufacturer, contact details for the manufacturer, product references and dimensions. At this stage, data may also be added for use during the construction phase - this can include the unit weight, packaging details and dimensions, planned installation dates, durations and commissioning dates. Stage 5 data, will consist of the actual installation information, commonly referred to as "as-built information". This can include actual installation dates, warranty start date, warranty duration, maintenance and inspection tasks, plus links to the product literature. At handover, the final pieces of data, such as commissioning information, will complete the data set.

VISUALIZING THE DATA

The model as a container for your data provides a framework for storing and organising your facility data.

As humans, lists of data don't usually mean much to us. A list of dates or manufacturers is just a list of information. We often rely on data visualizations or other applications to give meaning to our data.

Our visual building model provides other ways of visualizing data. Spaces can be highlighted to show areas requiring planned maintenance. Colour coding of the spaces, according to a timeline of when the maintenance is required, provides an intuitive way of understanding upcoming work activities and grouping them efficiently.

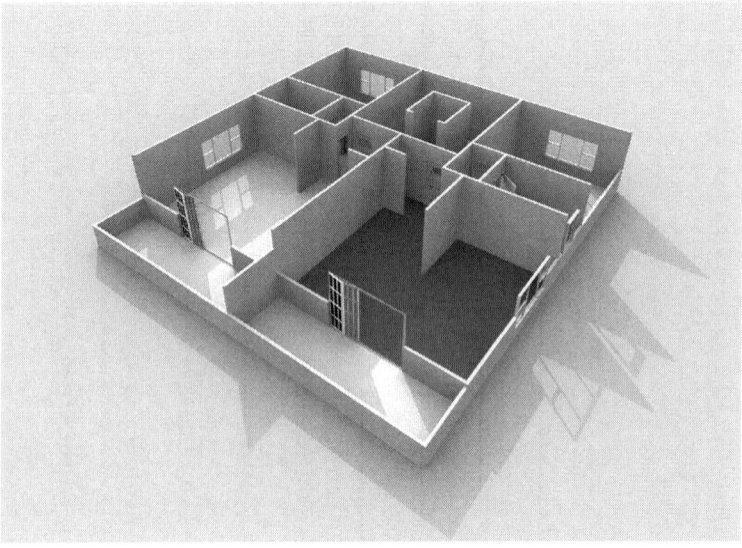

Some activities will require access equipment to ensure that a task can be carried out in a safe way. A visual model could also highlight other planned tasks that require access equipment, enabling the tasks to be grouped together provides an efficient use of the access equipment.

Using the model for data visualizations becomes a powerful tool for dynamic data. Dynamic data is constantly changing. Room sensors monitoring occupancy and temperature provide a continuous flow of information and dynamic data for an individual space can be linked directly with the model space. Dynamic data for a whole facility, such as energy consumption, can be linked to the whole facility or to any suitable container or element within the main facility master data container.

The data received from sensors can be monitored for acceptable ranges. If the temperature falls below a minimum allowed level or rises above a maximum allowed level, the spaces can be highlighted in a different colour.

This data could also be merged with occupancy data to visually identify possible links between continuous occupancy and high room temperatures.

The dynamic data possibilities include sensors that any facility would traditionally have, such as fire detection equipment, elevators, intruder alarms and energy monitoring. The IoT provides many more exciting and beneficial possibilities. Wifi access points could monitor the number of connected devices, which can provide an approximation of occupancy or activity. Environmental conditions such as outside temperatures, wind speed, wind direction and humidity can be compared with patterns of energy usage and internal temperatures. Flows of occupants through secure access points and how this relates to occupancy of communal areas can also be reviewed in order to make better informed decisions on facility usage, management and maintenance

Sensors are increasingly being added to major items of equipment within a building. Vibration and temperature sensors within air-handling units and boilers provide early warnings of future equipment failures. The sensors use machine learning to understand the data outputs that occur before a failure. These early warnings then alert the estate's management to carry out maintenance to prevent the impending failure. This means that your facility avoids expensive downtime, but also means that the maintenance is undertaken in a planned and managed approach, allowing parts to be ordered and the works to be scheduled to avoid inconveniencing your facility users.

MODEL-GENERATED DATA

The visual model - developed as a scaled representation of your facility - also provides its own source of data. The more accurate the model representation, the more accurate the data generated from the model will be.

Simple quantities and areas, such as floor areas, usable volumes and clear floor-to-ceiling heights, can be generated directly from your model. This information allows you to monitor changes to the model and any deviations from your design brief, providing accountability from your design team.

An accurate, quality model can generate quantities, volumes and areas of component materials. Material quantities are routinely used for estimating build costs through elemental breakdowns. As your design develops, the material quantities will become increasingly accurate as the individual components included within the model increase. This all adds to the reliability of the data, your awareness of any changes and the development of the design, which thereby helps protect your estate's development budget.

All models should have a base level of quality. Quality models will ensure that information generated from a model is accurate. Models should be assessed for their quality, either with a model quality checking report done by your design team, or with an independent quality check such as those provided by BIMsense.

2D INFORMATION

Another interesting feature of BIM is how it can be presented to make it appear familiar to users. 2D drawings, especially in the form of general arrangements that typically show floor layouts, are particularly common and familiar. BIM models can natively produce 2D layouts that appear identical to the traditional architectural layout drawings.

But, the 2D layouts that can be generated from BIM have significant benefits over the static paper of pdf equivalents. The layouts can be used for directly accessing information. Double clicking on a space can show the information related to the space, or take you to a 3D 360-degree view from within a room.

The model-generated 2D layouts can help with the navigation of the BIM model and with obtaining information about a space.

Such 2D layouts are dynamic. They can show exactly the information that you want them to display. If you want a particular door or door type displayed, these can be highlighted on the layout. If you want to show rooms that contain carpets, these can be highlighted on the layouts. The dynamically generated layouts are not only limited to the static model data, but can also display externally linked IoT dynamic data. Spaces where temperatures are above the acceptable range, for example, can be displayed in a different colour.

Consider the improved efficiency of an estate's hub or a command centre with multiple displays showing 2D model generated layouts, each displaying a different set of dynamic data, providing live and relevant information.

2D layouts are also useful for mobile and field devices. Mobile devices can often suffer from poor or limited connectivity. 2D layouts are lightweight, quick to generate and are often better for viewing on small devices while on the move.

HEALTH AND SAFETY

It is important that your model isn't just used as a more efficient way of working, but also makes your facility safer for your maintenance team and the people who use the building.

Your model, the master container for your data, can also be the way of organising health and safety risks.

Designers can add residual risks to the model as the design progresses. Residual risks are risks that will remain with a facility during its operational life. These are the risks that have not been eliminated during the design development process and will place operational restrictions of the finished building. If the controller for a fire damper is positioned at high level requiring an access scaffold tower to test the damper. The location of the fire damper introduces residual risk, as using a scaffold tower is a hazardous activity.

By adding residual risks to your building model you have a visual method of understanding the risks associated with your facility. It is also an efficient way that you and your design team can manage those risks. At the completion of each stage, you can assess the residual risks that can be accepted by your maintenance team and users of the building and identify unacceptable risks that you can eliminate through alternative designs.

Including residual risks within your model means you can view the exact locations where they occur. Atriums will be highlighted due to the risks associated with working at height and roof spaces can be highlighted as having insufficient edge protection. These spaces can be easily visualized using the model, creating an alternative method of managing a register of residual risks.

Risks can also be associated with activities and activities, like risks, can also be included within your data model containers. Each activity is a maintenance task that needs to be undertaken by someone in your estates team. This may introduce an inherent risk, such as working at height.

The risk is not continuously present, it will only occur while undertaking the maintenance task.

There will also be risks associated with assets within your estate, such as high-pressure gas lines, or certain types of cooling units with risks from legionella. All these items will have strategies in place to ensure that the likelihood of incidents is reduced, as long as they are maintained according to legislation and manufacturers' recommendations.

This provides another example of using your model as a data container beyond using it for initial design and construction information. It's unlikely that you will manage this data directly within your model, it's more likely that you will access and manage this information through specific applications that will allow you to visualize and manage your facility in a really proactive way.

DIGITAL DESIGN BRIEF

The digital design brief is discussed in detail later in Chapter 5, but it's worth understanding how a digital design brief becomes the starting point for your building model master data container.

A digital design brief provides the starting point for the data structure and the formal requirements, ensuring your project models are developed in such a way that they will become a suitable container for your data.

The digital design brief will be the primary source of information for your design team. When they need to check the required occupancy for a space, the digital design brief will be the place of reference. When they need to understand the data structure for each space, the digital design brief will provide the information. It will provide a data template.

By providing a digital design brief, we reduce the amount of data entry required from our designers. Data templates can be imported into the common design authoring tools. This enables designers to focus on developing innovative and effective design solutions rather than getting bogged down in the detail of setting up a data structure.

> *It's essential that all these new technologies and approaches provide objective benefits and are made as simple as possible to implement. Adding data to your model isn't an easy task. It needs to be made simple. Data templates simplify the process.*

MANAGING YOUR PROJECT

Collating and storing all your estate data in one place, in one container, will provide you with enormous benefits throughout your facility's operational life.

It will also provide benefits during the design and construction phase.

A quality, data-rich model will give you the opportunity to monitor the progress of the design in line with your digital design brief. Areas of non-compliance can be highlighted within the model and assessed for impacts.

Build costs can be monitored through automatically generated cost plans from the model data. This means the effects of changes and design decisions can be understood instantly. Additional linked data sets will allow long-term life cycle impacts to be assessed.

And by having a clear plan - your EIR - that sets out exactly what model information should be provided at what stage, you will be able to effectively and objectively monitor and report on progress.

If your EIR contains a data template, which we look at in Chapter 13: Employer's data requirements and BIM template, the model can be automatically checked for the inclusion of the required data at each project stage.

The deliverables from your design team are checked against their Task Information Delivery Plans (TIDPs). The TIDPs developed by your designers provide you with a schedule of the information that they will develop and the stages at which this information will be provided.

Areas with missing information are easily highlighted, so you can implement timely and effective measures to eliminate the root causes of problems and prevent a knock-on, critical effect on your project programme.

A well-defined data-rich model will reduce your project risks.

The risk of the design exceeding the budget, the risk of your project being delivered late and the risk of substandard quality are all reduced through a well-defined data-rich model.

The project models and the data within them also provide a reliable audit trail of the evolving data. The development of the models, the archived and current versions within your Common Data Environment, or CDE, provides a history of versions - what was added and when. Hopefully, you will never need to refer to the development of the data. But, it's useful to know that you can do this if a major problem occurs.

The early stages of a project are often focused on adding detail to an outline project brief. This involves consultations with end users, ensuring that their requirements and needs are fully understood and that the facility will meet those needs.

At the start of a project, your digital design brief will have areas where data is required to complete the brief. Incomplete items could include the number of power outlets within a space. To assess this, you will need to understand and record the use of the space, the number of occupants and the equipment that will be used in the space. This data can all add to the digital design brief data set. By having a single source of information, in a data model arrangement, you have an efficient way of cataloging and storing the data. Metadata can also be added to each decision point. Metadata is data about the data, such as whether end users were involved in a design decision, such as the location of fixed furniture, and the date the decision was made.

Any data missing from the digital design brief can be assessed at any stage of the project. Ideally, required decision dates will be added to each item. This will ensure decisions are planned earlier in the design process and made in a timely manner.

OBJECTIVE CHECKING

Developing digital design brief information enables full objective checking of the developing design model. The checking process can be automated or semi-automated, with the resultant actions directly managed within a digital task manager application. This frees up time so you and your team can focus on the big issues, critical design decisions that are preventing progress and are critical to the success of a project.

Project data should be stored within the model, or linked to relevant parts of the model, unless there is a good reason why this shouldn't happen. This data should be raw data, for instance, where a room has a maximum temperature requirement, it should be stored in an attribute as a number and not provided as a link to an external pdf data source. This is again in order to ensure relevant data cannot be lost due to ongoing information management outside of the model, such as on a Common Data Environment (CDE). The risk is that documents are moved to alternative files or renamed resulting in broken hyperlinks between the model and the relevant data.

There will of course be compromises and every project will have some unique requirements or unusual or legacy data. But, providing clear data requirements and responsibilities will reduce incorrect data formats. We also look at the detail of data formats in Chapter 13.

ROOM DATA SHEETS: UNDERSTANDING THE DATA WITHIN A MODEL

A room data sheet provides a good framework for understanding the data within a model. A traditional room data sheet contains information that defines a space such as the finishes, the furniture and the environmental conditions.

It's possible for a significant quantity of room data sheet information to be generated directly from the model, or through linked data sources. Some parts of a room data sheet are directly related to the space and this information will be associated with the space data container. The name of the space, room number, occupancy and environmental parameters would all be derived from model data. Area, perimeter and floor-to-ceiling heights are all calculated from geometric visual data. Then finally, equipment lists are developed from the items actually located and modelled within the space, the number of twin socket outlets is generated from the actual number located within the space.

The information for a room data sheet comes from the model. The presentation of the information can be tailored for your needs, individual sheets for each space or a full table of all the spaces and all the relevant attributes. But, the big advantage is that the room data sheet actually represents what has been designed. As a room size changes, the calculated area will change and this will be instantly available within a new room data sheet output, the information is fully coordinated.

CHAPTER SUMMARY

Your EIR should be in place from the very earliest stages of any project and definitely before your first designer is appointed.

- Think about your model as a container for data. The building is the master container, it has sub-containers such as spaces and individual object containers, such as light fitting, within the spaces. Data can be added to any of the containers. Think of the BIM model as the Russian doll of building data.

- An EIR is the plan for your model. You need to have this plan in place at the earliest possible stage of a project. It becomes more difficult to implement later as the quantity of data increases as a project progresses.

- Having data associated with your model enables visualizations in 2D and 3D environments.

- Models can be used for identifying, understanding and monitoring health and safety risks

- Your requirements should be developed using a digital approach, which will fully define your requirements, allow you to monitor progress, and enable objective and automated checking.

- Information, such as a room data sheets, should be contained and derived from your model, ensuring that your information is fully coordinated.

CHAPTER 3: A DATA-CENTRIC CULTURE

Culture - *The attitudes and behaviour characteristic of a particular social group. (Oxford Dictionaries)*

WHAT IS AN ORGANISATION'S CULTURE?

There are many different definitions of culture. Another Oxford Dictionaries definition, which is particularly relevant to organisations, is: "The ideas, customs and social behaviour of a particular people or society."

Culture isn't a documented collection of rules and procedures. The culture of an organisation, made up of a collection of people, is defined by the behaviour and actions of the people within it.

This means that what people actually do defines a culture, not what an organisation says it does, for example, if documented procedures aren't followed then the culture of an organisation is different from its documentation.

The culture or an organisation is important as it provides the implicit guidance on what to do and what is expected during our working day.

WHY SHOULD DATA BE PART OF AN ORGANISATION'S CULTURE?

Information, or data, informs everything we do, from a supermarket shop to a business purchase. Much of this information is contained within our brain, it has developed through the outcomes of previous actions, good and bad.

Organisational decisions are made by individuals using available and accessible information. When objective external information is not available and a quick decision is required, our decisions tend to be made using empirical data from our previous experiences.

But, if relevant data had been readily available, could the decisions have been better, would they have resulted in better outcomes?

There are clear examples of where not only can such data-driven decisions provide better outcomes, but they can also save lives. Malcolm Gladwell's Blink - The Power of Thinking Without Thinking, details an example from 1996 where Brendan Reilly at Cook County Hospital in the US, introduces a data-driven checklist to assess how to deal with patients with chest pains. The problem used to be that it was difficult to separate those who were having a heart attack and required urgent treatment from those who had another condition. Correctly identifying those with a heart attack would enable a hospital's limited resources to be directed at the most urgent patients.

The accuracy of assessing a patient using medical judgement alone resulted in a correct heart attack diagnosis 75%-89% of the time. But, by using a simple data-driven algorithm approach, correct diagnoses were increased to 95%, a significant improvement. The effect of this data remains in widespread use, correctly assessing heart attacks and saving lives every day.

The Cook County Hospital heart attack diagnosis produced significant benefits. In many cases the benefits may be small, but when all the outcomes are added together and compounded, by continually improving our decisions, the benefits are significant.

The data becomes valuable, it can improve outcomes that result in efficient ways of working, reduced costs and prevent wrong decisions.

Every organisation has enormous quantities of available information, from intangible collective knowledge to detailed expenditure records. Much of the information exists in isolated islands, such as a hard drive on someone's laptop, difficult to get hold of, difficult to interpret and with no ability for it to communicate effectively with information from other islands. A document containing the details of replacement parts for an automatic door opener, for example, may exist within a physical document. This is better than knowledge being held in someone's head, but accessing the information is time-consuming, and the information needs to be read and interpreted. If you need to order replacement parts, you need to manually transfer the information from the physical document to another system. In many circumstances, it's quicker and more effective to just order a whole replacement unit. But, that becomes a subjective decision based upon past experiences.

Information stored digitally as pdf files and made accessible improves the ease at which information can be obtained. But the information remains isolated and unable to talk to other information sources.

When we start to properly organise our information and structure our data, it becomes increasingly useful and increasingly easier to access. Spreadsheets, if maintained and developed correctly contain objective data. Although, as with pdfs, this type of information often remains isolated.

BIM and the data contained within models provides just one source and method for organising your information.

> *It is the development of an organisational culture that views all its data as valuable - and emphasises the methods of collecting and making data available - that will future proof your organisation.*

If everyone understands the importance of data, and takes actions to collect and use data in an open way, you will have a data-centric culture. It will make sure that everyone in your organisation is thinking about how data is collected, the format and its potential uses. And objective, evidence-based decisions will be made using the available data.

A Harvard Business review, The Evolution of Decision Making: How Leading Organizations are Adopting a Data-Driven Culture, (2012), states that organisations that can "make accurate and timely decision" can "identify challenges, spot opportunities, and adapt with agility".

The review conducted a global survey of 646 executives, managers and professionals across all industries and found that: "More than 70% of the organizations that had deployed analytics throughout their organizations reported improved financial performance, increased productivity, reduced risks, and faster decision making. Organizations with less widespread distribution of analytics access were typically 20 percentage points less likely to report such benefits."

HOW TO CREATE A DATA-CENTRIC CULTURE

It's not usually possible to force a cultural change, you can't just declare that data is now a central part of your organisation. As detailed above, culture is defined by an organisation's collective actions and behaviours. But, cultures do constantly change and evolve.

When looking to embed a data-centric culture, look for many small changes together with education on the benefits of BIM. Cultural change will require constant reinforcement of ideas, before ideas become widespread and habitual. You can do this by establishing advocates for data and BIM throughout your organisation who will work with you to spread the culture of data.

> *At BIMsense we have worked with organisations from medium-sized contractors through to the largest universities in the UK, and have witnessed successful data-centric cultural changes.*

It's really useful to have peer endorsement of the ideas and methods that you are trying to spread. But, don't worry about changing everybody. You will never be able to introduce something new that everyone will buy into, just accept that. Not everyone will "get" an organisation's culture. Aim to reach a tipping point where you have enough advocates and enough momentum for cultural change to actively happen. People tend to like to fit within social groups. As they adopt the dominant behaviours of an organisation, these become the expected behaviours that define the culture.

There will always be those individuals who will jump on board for a new idea, these are often referred to as innovators. I'm guessing that you are probably an innovator. Innovators won't need to see the evidence of positive outcomes from something new, such as data within models. They are excited by new ideas, excited by the potential benefits and will want to be involved in driving new ideas forward. You should initially target this type of person, they will become your fellow BIM advocates.

The next group of people are the early adopters. They will need to see some evidence of the benefits of BIM. They will need to know the answers to questions such as what can it actually do, what benefits will provide and what the costs are. But, armed with the evidence, early adopters will want to use BIM for the benefits that it provides.

Once your innovators and early adopters are using and benefiting from BIM, the late adopters within your organisation will get on board. Many late adopters will have been sceptical about BIM, and will have found it difficult to understand how BIM could provide benefits. But, as the number of BIM advocates within your organisation increases, the evidence of the benefits will also increase. This raises social pressure to change, bringing a fear of missing out. Change will require effort and at the beginning, especially for the late adopters, the learning curve will appear too steep. As soon as your late adopters start embracing BIM, the cultural norms for making data a central requirement will have been set. Your organisation will have gone through a digital transformation.

Finally you have your laggards. There will always be some people who won't understand why BIM and data are important. Perhaps they won't see the benefits of change, or their existing habits are too deeply embedded. Whatever the reason, just accept that you won't be able to change everyone.

DEVELOPING A DATA-CENTRIC CULTURE

There is a dilemma here: people find it difficult to understand what data can do unless they have the data and it's presented in a visual way. But, at the start, when making decisions about what data to have, you won't have any examples to understand the benefits and what it can do.

SAMPLE DATA

Sample data provides a really useful understanding of model data. It can help others to visualize what the data can do and see how it can help your organisation. The sample data would ideally be added to an earlier BIM model from your estate, this could be from a previous project where one of your designers developed a model. Early models generally consisted of reasonably good visual models, but lacked structured and comprehensive data. Although, such a model should be good enough for the purpose of setting up sample data.

Existing models can be used as a starting point for sample data and have the benefit of representing a familiar physical asset. If you don't have a model from an earlier project then any model will do. There are a variety of sources where models are available to be used for sample purposes, such as:

- An early version of your proposed facility - this may not have sufficient components to enable you to effectively add data (there probably won't be any monitoring and evaluation, for example).

- A model that you have from an earlier scheme - you should check that the model is suitable for adding data. Have you been provided with the models for the scheme? Do you have all the designers' models? If not, can you ask your designers or contractors for the model? Check that the model contains sufficient detail, especially manageable components.

- A model from another organisation - the models here are likely to be well defined and suitable for use. But clearly the models will not be as relevant.

I have provided some links to the sources of sample models at the end of this chapter. The links are external, so please ensure that any models are suitable for your needs and do not have any licensing restrictions.

Various tools can be used for adding sample data to a model. At BIMsense, we use various tools, including simplebim and bespoke Python scripts, but you could use any model authoring tool.

I always recommend using the buildingSMART IFC format for your models and data. Formed in 1995, buildingSMART is an industry backed not-for-profit community developing open standards. buildingSMART lists the following benefits of the open IFC format:

- More transparent, collaborative and open workflows.
- Greater information certainty due to a shared vocabulary of industry terms.
- More open procurement processes.
- Processes that are inclusive for companies large and small.
- Greater re-use of data; less re-keying of the same data.
- Easier integration with linked data and created in related industries.

And notes the following:

Open, shareable information unlocks more efficient, transparent and collaborative ways of working throughout the entire life cycle of buildings and infrastructure. The growing adoption of new asset delivery processes, such as building information modelling (BIM) also allows owners and operators of built assets, working with their service partners, to plan their capital investments and understand the likely whole-life costs of maintaining and using those assets for their intended purposes. (BuildingSMART)

IFC also provides you with long-term data security. If you were to only use a proprietary vendor developed format, then you depend upon the organisation that owns the format to continue to provide support. For most profit-making organisations, support for a legacy format will only be provided if there is a sound business case, taking into account factors such as profit, risk and the organisational vision. Using IFC format will mean that you won't be tied to a proprietary format, which should maximise the life and long-term security of your data.

If you want to use a proprietary model authoring tool, such as Autodesk Revit or ArchiCAD, then the key here is to save your sample model in both the native file format (for Revit files they have .rvt extension) and in the IFC file format (the file extension is .ifc).

I will continue to look into the detail of IFC throughout this book and at the end of this chapter you can find links to download an outline data structure relevant to your needs.

The sample data should be relevant to your anticipated needs. If you need data to plan the maintenance of your facility, then you will need information to select maintainable assets, together with planned maintenance activities. If you want to have space data, then you will need your spaces to be classified and to contain data such as planned occupancy. At this sample data stage, none of this data has to be accurate, it's just providing awareness and understanding. But, the more accurate the data, the more relevant and beneficial your sample model will be.

TOOLS FOR SHOWING YOUR SAMPLE MODEL

A sample model, with sample data, is a great way to learn about the possibilities of a model and for spreading awareness of the benefits of BIM.

To maximise the benefits of your sample model, you will need to be able to present and display the types of uses you can get from the model and the benefits for each use.

To do this, you will need some tools for manipulating the data. Where possible, these tools should be available to your wider team, so once you have wowed your team with the possibilities of BIM, they can take it further and experiment with their own specific uses.

BIM applications and tools are available in a mixture of formats, licensing options, application types and costs. You should select something suitable for your short-term needs with the understanding that what you are attempting to do here is to change your organisational culture and obtain buy-in from your colleagues, but, this may also link into a long-term software solution. If you are super efficient and organised in developing your sample model, the trial periods that is offered by most of the software options may be sufficient.

With this in mind, I have selected some of the more useful options. In many cases, you will require at least two software solutions, a tool to input your data and a tool to manipulate your data. The list is by no means definitive and there will, at least for the foreseeable future, be a steady stream of new applications.

The subject of selecting software solutions is beyond the scope of this book, but hopefully the information below is enough information for you to make short-term solutions using free trial software. As such, I have provided the following information for each potential software application:

- Name of the software tool and the organisation.
- An overview of the uses of the tool (focused on the uses for the developing a BIM culture, not the full remit of uses of the software), together with pros and cons.
- Licensing options, costs and any restrictions.

They have been sorted into three categories: software that enables the enriching and altering of model data; software for manipulating and extracting data, and software for visualizing and viewing the data. Prices correct at time of publication (2018).

SAMPLE SOFTWARE FOR ENRICHING AND ALTERING MODEL DATA

Simplebim - Windows desktop application

Description: Manipulating data, enriching data. Data can be manipulated directly within the graphical interface or through Excel spreadsheet templates. The spreadsheet templates are the most efficient way of adding large volumes of data. But, it can be a steep learning curve to understand your way around them.

Free Trial period: 30 days.

Licensing cost: From €800 for a full single-user licence, to €2,500+VAT for a commercial network licence.

FME Desktop - Windows desktop application, can be implemented in various ways, including a server environment

Description: Manipulating data, setting data rules. File formats and data are manipulated using data graphs. The software isn't specific to BIM or IFC data. Its main use is for setting up rules for the automatic manipulation of data. Not one that I would recommend for developing non-critical sample data.

Trial period: 30 days, with a developer option for perpetual non-commercial use.

Licensing cost: Various full licensing options starting with a single user. Prices range from £1,700 for a Professional Edition, up to £5,400+VAT for a Smallworld Edition.

Revit from Autodesk - Windows desktop application

Description: Model authoring software, for adding data to graphical components. Marketed as software in which to enable BIM, Revit is an intelligent model-based process to plan, design, construct and manage buildings and infrastructure. Revit supports a multidiscipline process for collaborative design.

Trial period: 30 days.

Licensing cost: £2,460+VAT for an annual stand-alone single-user licence.

ArchiCAD from Nemetscheck - Windows desktop application

Description: Model authoring software, adding data to graphical components.

Trial period: 30 days.

Licensing cost: Solo packages start from £1,799.00 +VAT, or £120.00 +VAT per month, which includes a perpetual software licence, energy evaluation, a range of 2D detailing objects (roof tiles, brick and block), a localised template and a minimum 12-months service agreement for upgrades and support.

MANIPULATING AND EXTRACTING DATA

Solibri

Description: As the leading BIM validation product on the market, Solibri offers: advanced clash detection and management; the ability to automatically analyse and group clashes according to severity; quick and easy detection of relevant problems; and deficiency detection. At BIMsense, it's our preferred tool for assessing and analysing models. However, it is an advanced tool that can be difficult to understand and use without training. It also has a limited trial period of only two weeks.

Trial period: 14 days.

Licensing cost: First year subscription is included in the licence price at £6,400+VAT.

BIMsync

Description: Share, visualize and collaborate on BIM models, issues, documents and drawings in your browser. No plugins or installation needed, runs directly within a browser. Access can be provided to multiple users. Model data can be queried and exported to Excel. Due to the browser interface, detailed analysis can sometimes be a little slow. It doesn't have the advanced options available within Solibri.

Trial period: 14 days.

Licensing cost: Price on application. Pricing is dependant upon project size and number of users.

SimpleBIM

See details above in Sample software for enriching and altering model data.

Revit

See details above in Sample software for enriching and altering model data.

ArchiCAD

See details above in Sample software for enriching and altering model data.

VIEWING THE DATA

Excel

Description: We all know Excel by now, don't we?! But just in case, it is a spreadsheet developed by Microsoft that features calculation, graphing tools and pivot tables. I have added it here because of how familiar it is. It does now offer cloud options through Office 365, but these aren't as good as those offered through Google Sheets.

Trial period: You probably already have it but, if not, it's available as part of the Office 365 suite on a one-month trial basis. Alternatively, there are some great free spreadsheet alternatives such as Google Sheets and Open Office.

Licensing cost: A basic Office 365 subscription costs £79.99 per year.

Solibri

See details above in Manipulating and extracting data.

BIMsync

See details above in Manipulating and extracting data.

DATA USES

You will need to find practical examples of how the data can be used and the benefits that it can provide to enable your organisation to develop a data culture. The more the data is used and understood, the more it will become integral to your organisation. As it becomes understood, new ways of working with the data will be developed throughout your team. This will lead onto obtaining new sources of data and providing new integrations with new and existing applications.

Here are some examples of data uses:

- A schedule of room areas from the model can be used to:
    - Compare previous revisions of the model with the latest version.
    - Sort room areas into departments, faculties or room types.
    - Add colour coding to provide visual representations of large rooms.
    - Determine the overall cost of the building at a m2 rate (using both forecast and actual costs).
    - Identify the in-use energy costs of the building compared with a m2 rate.

- Occupancy rate and space usage data can be used to:
    - Sort the rooms for m2 per designed occupant (this is also a key performance indicator, or KPI, in higher education).
    - Colour code within the model areas of high occupancy, and check how this is distributed throughout the building.
    - Sort and view spaces for room use rates and locations.

- Occupancy and sufficient furniture data can tell you:
    - Whether each space has sufficient desks and chairs for the planned number of occupants?
    - If the desks and chairs are arranged to enable access?

- Analyse the ratio of occupied spaces compared with non-occupied spaces:
    - How does this compare to good practice?
    - Is the design efficient?

- Begin some reasonably complex analysis, such as:
    - Floor finishes, what is the anticipated life of each type of floor finish?
        - What would the cost benefit be of improving a floor finish by using one with a longer-life?
        - What are the cleaning regimes (and associated costs) for each floor finish?

- Analyse your energy uses, depending upon your submetering arrangement, such as:
    - Lighting - what is the average daily use? How efficient are the current lights? What would the cost benefit be of changing light fittings?

CHAPTER SUMMARY

An organisation needs to place data at the centre of its culture, this requires a change in behaviours and actions. BIM is a key data resource for an organisation with a large estate.

SAMPLE MODEL STEPS

Developing a sample model provides a meaningful way of changing beliefs about the benefits of BIM. The steps to developing your sample model:

- Select a model. Ideally, this is a model from a previous project in your estate. Otherwise, try to obtain a model that has some relevance to your organisation.

- Enhance the sample model with data. Add data that is relevant, if you have a maintenance team, add maintenance data. Refer to the Chapter 13 for the format of the data.

- Experiment with the model. Export schedules, ask questions and obtain answers through the data. Find out what problems your colleagues encounter and explore ways to make their lives easier.

- Present the benefits. Show examples of what BIM can do and how it can make someone's job easier. Try to be specific and solve existing problems.

SAMPLE MODEL SOURCES

- East Dormitory Test Files
  From Prairie Sky Consulting, IFC and RVT files.

- OpensourceBIM test files
  From opensourcebim.org, IFC files.

- Schependomlaan
  From openBIMstandards, IFC files.

- Various model files
  From The University of Auckland, Open IFC Model Repository, IFC files.

- Revit sample files
  From Autodesk, RVT files.

- Free sample files
  From Enscape, RVT files.

- Various model files
  From grabcad.com, mainly RVT files (type revit into the search box).

Always check the terms of the licence and the suitability of the models.

CHAPTER 4: ESTABLISHING YOUR ORGANISATIONAL DATA REQUIREMENTS

Requirement - *A thing that is needed or wanted. A thing that is compulsory; a necessary condition. (Oxford Dictionaries)*

In Chapter 2, we touched on the importance of Employer's Information Requirements (EIR) for a project and later we have a full chapter that details all of the parts of EIR. One of the most important reasons for having an EIR is so you can set out your exact data requirements. The first step is to establish exactly what data you require.

BIM LEVEL 2 GUIDANCE DOCUMENTS

Before we go into the detail of how to establish your organisational data requirements, it's worth just having a quick refresher on the BIM Level 2 framework and the available guidance documents.

In Chapter 1 - Introduction, I briefly made reference to the UK government's BIM Level 2 mandate and how the mandate provided a useful push for the implementation of BIM in a structured way.

A large part of the BIM Level 2 mandate revolves around published guidance documents. These primarily consist of British Standards (BS) and Publicly Available Specifications (PAS). Both types of documents are published by the British Standards Institution (BSI). A PAS is a standard that responds to a rapidly developing industry need and is produced to provide immediate structure and guidance, which absolutely applied to BIM.

It's the intention of the BSI that any published PAS is replaced by a BS code of practice within two years, with the BS code of practice providing robust guidance and processes.

However, we are currently in the position where the first BIM PAS was published in 2013 and others published in 2014 and 2015, but none of these have yet been republished as a BS code of practice. We are also expecting two new BIM PAS guidance documents in 2018.

The current suite of BIM Level 2 guidance published by BSi consists of:

BS 1192:2007 + A2:2016: *Collaborative production of architectural, engineering and construction information.* This is the original collaborative working document from which the other documents are based. It provides the guidance on common naming, including file naming.

PAS 1192-2:2013: *Specification for information management for the capital/delivery phase of construction projects using building information modelling.* This deals with the construction (CAPEX) phase, and specifies the requirements for BIM Level 2 maturity. It sets out the framework, roles and responsibilities for collaborative BIM working; builds on the existing standard of BS 1192, and expands the scope of the Common Data Environment.

PAS 1192-3: 2014: *Specification for information management for the operational phase of assets using building information modelling (BIM).* This deals with the operational (OPEX) phase, focusing on use and maintenance of an Asset Information Model.

BS 1192-4: 2014: *Collaborative production of information. Fulfilling employer's information exchange requirements using the Construction Operations Building Information Exchange (COBie).* This guidance document was published straight to a BS code of practice. It provides detail on the requirements of a COBie deliverable. It also contains employer purposes which we look at in more detail in this chapter.

PAS 1192-5: 2015: *Specification for security-minded building information modelling, digital built environments and smart asset management.* This document provides guidance on managing the security of information and detail. It also provides a method for assessing the security level or sensitivity of assets.

BS 8536-1:2015: *Briefing for design and construction. Code of practice for facilities management (buildings infrastructure).* This document provides a framework for ensuring that a building's design fully considers the needs of the end users. One of the key points of this guidance is the involvement of the end users - including those responsible for the management of a facility - at the earliest design stages, to try to ensure that a facility meets expectations. BS 8536-2:2016 code of practice also provides similar guidance for linear infrastructure assets, such as roads and utilities.

PAS 1192-6: *Specification for collaborative sharing and use of structured health and safety information using BIM.* This document introduces the use of the project model (or outputs from the project model such as COBie) as a method for managing health and safety information.

All of the above documents can be downloaded for free from bim-level2.org.

The following specification is due for release:

PAS 1192-7: *Specification for defining and maintaining structured digital product information used for the design, construction and use of a product or built asset.* It has a remit of providing guidance on a consistent approach to product information, i.e. the information contained within a digital object.

Some of the above documents also refer to other documents and other sources of information that expand the reach of the BIM Level 2 mandate. Uniclass 2015, Government Soft Landings and the BIM Protocol from the Construction Industry Council are among the many referenced sources of supporting information.

CONSTRUCTION OPERATIONS AND BUILDING INFORMATION EXCHANGE (COBIE)

COBie provides a method for exchanging information in a structured format.

In the past couple of years, a lot of opinions and commentary have been shared on the benefits and disadvantages of COBie and I don't want to add to the noise.

The development of your organisational information neither requires nor precludes the use of COBie. So if you want to rigidly follow BIM Level 2 guidance and have COBie as a deliverable this can be obtained but, equally, COBie is not required for the development of your organisational information.

To understand why this is the case, let's have a very brief look into COBie, the facts.

COBie provides data in a structured way. The usual way of providing COBie is through a spreadsheet XML 2003 format, which can be considered a standard spreadsheet. COBie is often described as a subset of an information model. This means it contains a defined and limited set of model information, the data within the model. This is an important point, as the larger set of data for which COBie is a subset is your IFC model. COBie has a predefined mapping (or links) between IFC-defined entities and attributes (the individual items of data).

So, it's a relatively simple approach to produce a COBie spreadsheet from your data model, should it be required. But, you also have the advantage of having a model with a richer and more comprehensive set of data than can be delivered through COBie alone.

It's also possible to do bespoke mapping from COBie to IFC. However, by having your data arranged in a compliant IFC structure, this should be limited and possibly not required at all.

My advice is to let the conversation around COBie continue, don't get sucked in. And should you require COBie, which could be useful to simplify the import of data into your Computer Aided Facilities Management (CAFM) system, then rest easy that this can be achieved.

DATA REQUIREMENTS

The data requirements for an individual project will not be entirely unique. Your Organisational Information Requirements (OIR), a term from PAS 1192-3, will establish the data requirements of your organisation. OIRs are looked at in more detail in Chapter 12 - Organisational and Asset Information Requirements OIR and AIR.

In this chapter, I will focus specifically on developing your data requirements for your model. I won't, at this stage, be looking at the specific nature or detail of the data, this is covered in Chapter 13: Employer's data requirements and BIM data template. Instead, I will detail here the different data purposes and the types of data that will be required to fulfil a purpose.

Establishing your organisational data requirement from scratch will not be easy and it's a task that will continue throughout the lifetime of your facility. An organisation's data needs and uses will continually evolve as data maturity increases and new technology becomes available.

You will have many different uses for facilities and estates data within the different departments of your organisation. A space planning department within a university organisation already has detailed information on staff and student numbers, together with timetabling and space information. The maintenance team has information on equipment that requires regular replacement or servicing and the organisation's strategic planning team has information on anticipated future needs and the condition of the buildings within an estate.

To fully establish your organisational data requirements, you will need to involve all your departments. Each will have its own unique - and often complex - data needs and requirements. One of the ways you can provide your team with the tools to understand their data requirements is by developing a data culture, which we looked at in Chapter 3: A data-centric culture.

GETTING STARTED WITH BS 1192-4 - EMPLOYER PURPOSES

A useful starting point, when establishing your data requirements, is to use a framework of data purposes.

BS 1192-4, the BSI code of practice for collaborative production of information, provides one such framework, referred to as employer purposes.

1. The employer purposes are:
2. Register
3. Support for business questions
4. Support for compliance and regulatory responsibilities
5. Management of capacity and utilisation
6. Management of security and surveillance
7. Support for repurposing
8. Predicted and actual impacts
9. Operations
10. Maintenance and repair
11. Replacement
12. Decommissioning and disposal

Employer purposes provide focus on the reason why you are obtaining data. You have a specific need and you obtain data to fulfill your need, rather than obtaining data because of some anticipated future need. Data has a cost, obtaining data from your supply chain will have a cost and maintaining your data will have a cost. You need to be very specific about the data you are going to obtain and its purpose so that you can justify its quantity and its value.

There are other sources to use as starting points for developing your estate's data requirements, for example PAS 1192-3 provides, within Annex A, a schedule of activities that "may assist"' in developing your information requirements.

But, the 11 employer purposes cover most of the common operational-phase data uses - the data you will use while your building is in use - and keeps the list focused and concise, which is especially useful in the early stages of developing your data requirements.

You should also consider data that will be of use during the design and delivery phase. This should not just be data useful to contractors during construction, although a well-developed and quality-checked model will be useful to all project stakeholders. It should also include data that enables you to track build costs, risks and design development.

DATA MAINTENANCE COSTS

The cost of maintaining data is often overlooked or underestimated, and is explained in more detail in Chapter 10: Data maintenance.

Practically every physical asset requires maintenance of some form, whether that is planned maintenance, reactive maintenance, upgrading or planned replacement - an asset will not remain useful if it has not been maintained. If you don't maintain your physical assets they will become damaged, irreparable or obsolete. If you apply this principle to your house, a house over many years if not maintained will eventually decay and crumble. But, if well maintained, your house will be your home and potentially the home for many families for centuries to come.

This maintenance principle applies beyond physical assets into non-physical assets such as data.

Your data will require maintenance. As an example, if not maintained, data from the 1990s will have been kept on data storage devices that are no longer supported - remember floppy disks, anyone? In addition, the format of the data may become obsolete and commercial organisations often only provide support for their software applications for a limited time. And the data itself will most likely also require regular updates. A register of employees, for example, will need to be updated as employees join and leave an organisation.

Organisations are beginning to consider data as a valuable asset similar to any physical assets, with Individuals or teams are being employed as data or information managers to ensure the governance and long-term reliability of their valuable data.

When considering your organisational employer purposes, don't just focus on what you need, also consider what you don't need and the reasons why you will not require certain data. This promotes ownership of the decisions by ensuring that reasons are considered for collecting information and equally reasons why information is not required..

It's useful to understand each of the employer purposes in detail. They will provide you will the language to articulate some of the key potential data uses to your team.

The text in quotation marks comes directly from **BS 1192-4** - the BSI's code of practice for the collaborative production of information.

1: REGISTER

"Register of assets to support accurate auditing and reporting" - BS 1192-4

Register is the very starting point for collecting facility data. If you require any type of asset data you will require a register of your assets. The register employer purpose is mandatory if any of the other employer purposes apply to your organisation.

"A register of assets should be provided to support accurate auditing and reporting. This should include both spatial and physical assets and their groupings." - BS 1192-4

Your register of assets should include items such as light fittings and air-handling units, as well as spaces such as rooms, floors and the overall facility itself.

"Every named inside or outside Space (location) should be documented along with every distinct Floor (region) containing them. The Zones defining public/private access should be documented, along with other Zones as required." - BS 1192-4

Zones are useful for grouping together similar spaces or spaces used for a particular purpose. Zones can also overlap, in a similar way to a Venn diagram. All the spaces for an English department can be contained within their own zone, which will include departmental classrooms and admin spaces. The classrooms can also be contained within a classroom zone. As with a Venn diagram, there is an overlapping area of the two zones.

MANAGEABLE COMPONENTS

"Every manageable Component should be documented along with every distinct functional System whether containing manageable Components or not, and every distinct product Type defining the manageable Components including both generic and specific product and materials."
- BS 1192-4

Manageable components are assets that will require some form of management. This usually involves planned and preventative maintenance by your team. But, manageable components could also be assets that are used for monitoring, such as access control items.

The concept of manageable components is really useful when considering the data that you want to be collected. Not every component within a facility will require data. A concrete column will not generally require any form of maintenance during the lifetime of a facility. And if something does not require maintenance, why go to the expense and trouble of collecting and maintaining such information? A common approach is to exclude superfluous data from your final delivered dataset. This way, you avoid unnecessarily large datasets and unnecessary work for the custodians of the data model.

All registered assets will require classifying or grouping. By classifying, you reduce the dependence on consistent naming as a way of searching for similar types of assets. You can also apply a classification to the type of facility as a whole, to the use of spaces and to groupings of individual components into connected or related systems. There is more on Classifications in Chapter 8 and I will continue to touch on its importance throughout this book.

TYPICAL DATA FOR REGISTER

The data that should be provided for each employer purpose is not explicitly prescribed and neither should it be, you need some flexibility to make sure your data meets your requirements.

However, there are some general rules and typical data that will normally be required for this purpose.

As standard, names, classifications and descriptions should be provided for your facility, along with the floors, zones, all spaces, systems and assets.

The remaining items of data that can be provided to satisfy your requirement to obtain a register of your facility and assets becomes more subjective, and depend on your specific data uses, such as:

- **Facility:** Additional data for your facility can include global location data, such as coordinates and the address.

- **Floors:** Data you might require for each floor includes the height of the floor above a standard baseline (normally the floor level at the main entrance) and the clear height for each floor, excluding installations such as building services and ceilings, as this information can be included for each individual space.

- **Zones:** Zones consist of a collection of spaces. So for a zone to be any use you will need the standard items listed above, zone names, a description of the zones and a classification of the group. Then each relevant space will be assigned to a zone.

- **Spaces:** Spaces will need to include the standard information name, description and classification attributes mentioned above. There's a large amount of useful information that can be added to each individual space. But, for the purpose of providing a register of the space, it's usually limited to net and gross floor areas, together with the clear height within the room. The clear height will depend upon the finishes within a space.

For spaces without ceilings, the clear height should be calculated to the underside of the lowest building services within the space, but where ceilings or ceiling rafts are the lowest fixed element, these should form the basis of the clear height dimension. Areas and clear height dimensions should all be calculated directly from the model, not from manually entered dimensions.

And should the installed dimensions be different from the designed dimensions, then the model should be updated to represent the actual installation. Don't start fudging the information, it tends to lead to more and more fixes, which will lead to questions over the validity of your data.

- **Systems:** Systems are made up of a group of components, which may be connected together. The components that make up a building's mechanical ventilation can be grouped together into a system. Often, systems such as mechanical ventilation will be sub-grouped to provide additional information, which is useful for managing the facility. It's also possible to group components that do not form a continuous system, these tend to be non-building services components such as doors and windows. However, the benefits to linking such components are more limited, especially when considering that classification of components provides an equally effective way of grouping components. Some modelling authoring tools only allow building services to be added to systems. So, initially, only consider systems for building services components. As with zones, systems will tend to use just the standard data requirements. Each system will have a unique name, a description and a classification.

- **Assets:** Individual assets are variously referred to as components, entities or objects. Each of these will also have a type. Types enable common component information to be grouped together. As an example, some doors within a facility could be grouped together as a type 1. A type 1 door could be a 30-minute fire door, single swing, 2110 x 910mm. This information (including other data such as the manufacturer) will all be contained within the type. The individual occurrence of a type 1 door will contain more limited data such as the location of the door. Therefore, for an asset, register information will contain unique name, description and classification data.

Asset register data will also often include additional attributes such as asset type (fixed or loose), dimensional data, outline products data (such as colour and finish), dimensions and manufacturer and product number or references.

2: SUPPORT FOR BUSINESS QUESTIONS

"The employer should specify if information is required to support the evaluation of the business case for ownership and operation of the Facility. This should include continuous development of the Impacts and of the beneficial aspects of the Facility from the earliest deliverable onwards." - BS 1192-4

The business case for the ownership and operation of a facility can be evaluated from the earliest stages of design right through to ongoing evaluation during the operational phase. As detailed information becomes available, this should be included in the evaluation, providing greater certainty and reassurance. The business case should be evaluated throughout the life of the facility, with updated information that could include energy costs, maintenance costs and rental rates.

This employer purpose is all about structuring and obtaining data to provide objective information for the business case of your facility.

There will clearly be a need for such data during the design phase of a project, it's important to assess the ongoing project budgets and compare these to the original budgets that formed the original business case. But, business case assessments should also continue through to the operational phase of a facility. It's important to assess when a facility no longer provides value for money and your operations can be better served through a replacement building. At some point, the negatives of an older facility will outweigh the investment costs and outcomes of a new facility. Unplanned reactive maintenance, replacement of individual assets and systems, inefficient systems and an outdated design that no longer serves the intended functions could all contribute to this.

Having this data readily available will make the continual assessment of your facilities a possibility. The task could also be automated or semi-automated to provide a regular report that classifies and ranks your facilities based upon value for money.

WHAT TYPE OF DATA IS REQUIRED TO HELP MAKE BUSINESS CASE DECISIONS?

The data here can be wide and varied depending upon the inputs required to make your business case.

Many business case questions are focused around floor areas and usable areas, such as the space provided per user or per department, and comparisons of usable and ancillary spaces. Much of the data collected for the register will be useful for these types of questions. Floor areas, net and gross, are provided through the combination of individual spaces and spaces can be grouped by type, department, faculty and business unit (or any other required grouping) through classifications and zones. Additional information on the usage of space can include occupancy and utilisation..

Business case data also links back to costs, such as actual ongoing costs, including energy usage, cleaning costs and rents, or predicted future costs, such as planned maintenance, replacement of assets as they reach their end of life and anticipated increases of ongoing costs due to inflation, legislation and supply and demand.

Your model can include asset data such as anticipated life, replacement costs and a programme of planned maintenance activities. This will give you an objective measure of the costs of maintaining assets within your facility. This information can also be used during the design phase to evaluate the benefits of installing different types of assets according to anticipated life cycles, maintenance requirements and capital costs.

Planned and actual energy use can be linked to the facility as a whole. However, external and dynamic data is often better residing outside of the model, with the option of providing links to the data.

Some of the data required to assess your business case will not come from your facility model. But, by evaluating your data requirements and understanding exactly what questions you require answering, you develop a clear understanding of what you will need. You can then put a plan in place for obtaining that information.

3: SUPPORT FOR COMPLIANCE AND REGULATORY RESPONSIBILITIES

"The employer should specify if information is required to support the maintenance of the health and safety of the users of the Facility such as construction design and management (CDM) Issues." - BS 1192-4

This employer purpose links closely with PAS 1192-6 - Specification for collaborative sharing and use of structured hazard and risk information for health and safety. It also overlaps with many of the other employer purposes. If maintenance and repair information is required, it should include maintenance that is essential to regulatory compliance, for example, Legionella codes of practice.

"Issues should be related to named assets but might also be related to Attributes, Documents or Impacts." - BS 1192-4

Issues can also be interpreted as risks. For instance, the changing of a lamp at a high level has an associated risk. The changing of the lamp may also be a maintenance activity, we have a separate employer purpose for 'maintenance and repair', this leaves this employer purpose to focus on items such as risk.

The Construction (Design and Management) Regulations 2015 (CDM) ensure that health and safety issues are managed throughout a project, with the intention that risks are identified and then either reduced or eliminated. The identified risks should include those that are present during the construction of a facility and those that remain during the life of the facility (often referred to as residual risks).

Risk, especially health and safety risks is an important area and your model is ideally suited for the management of risks, so we take a deeper look at risk in Chapter 9.

"Jobs covering safety and security procedures and cautions within those safety procedures should be documented for handover." - BS 1192-4

A job can also be referred to as a task. It is possible that a task may have both a health and safety requirements and be a maintenance activity. Such as the activities required to reduce the risks associated with Legionella.

DATA TO MEET HEALTH AND SAFETY LEGAL REQUIREMENTS

Health and safety within any organisation is always (and quite rightly) given the highest priority. As such it makes sense that you should always aim to obtain health and safety information within your model. Although, there may be circumstances where this is not possible, for example members of your design team may not have a sufficient level of BIM competency to reliably add health and safety data to your model, or they may have equally effective alternative methods for managing the data.

Every organisation has a duty to remain legal. Adding this information to your BIM deliverables provides a way of making this task easier.

All life-safety systems, including fire alarms and fire doors, should be regularly inspected and tested at least every six months. The testing and inspection for all life safety systems can be added as tasks.

Much of this data will be collected through the maintenance and repair data purpose. However, if you want to concentrate only on maintaining those assets for which you have a legal duty, this employer purpose provides a more focused approach.

Even if you do require all the maintenance data for all your manageable assets, then it's useful to be able to understand maintenance activities that have a legal duty. This will require an additional data attribute, this could be a simple legal duty "yes/no" type question.

RESIDUAL RISKS

Residual risks are the risks that will remain with a facility throughout its operational life. These are the risks that have been catalogued but not eliminated during the design development process.

As a client for a project you should be aware of the residual risks associated with your new facility. The users and the maintenance team will have to live with and manage the risks throughout the life of the facility. Therefore, being able to understand, track and obtain organisational acceptance for the residual risks is an essential part of developing and delivering a project.

Risks within your model can be included as Industry Foundation Classes (IFC) property sets. We will look at the concept of property sets in detail in Chapter 13. But, for now it's sufficient to understand that the data associated with a risk can be grouped together and the grouping is called a property set. The IFC risk property has a defined name, Pset_Risk. The risk property set enables you to collate all significant risks and hazards within your model and manage those risks and hazards until ideally they are eliminated or reduced to an acceptable level.

4: MANAGEMENT OF CAPACITY AND UTILISATION

"Documentation of the intended capacity and utilization of the Facility should be provided as it is required to support comparisons of actual use and utilization and portfolio management." - BS 1192-4

Comparisons of planned and actual occupancy, and utilisation, provide a meaningful way of evaluating the design of a facility compared with the actual use. This prompts questions such as, why do we have a difference and how can we learn from this difference?

As with the IFC risk property set that can be used for residual risks, we also have an IFC property set that can be used for the management of capacity and utilisation employer purpose. The property set (which is referred to as *Pset_SpaceOccupancyRequirements*) includes standard data fields (or attributes) for the planned occupancy, the times during which a space will be occupied and the minimum area required for each occupant.

Having this information within your model allows easy access to the data, which is provided in a logical way. For example, data about a space, such as the designed occupancy of a space, is associated directly with the relevant space. This data can be made even more useful when combining with other data such as types of spaces or locations of spaces and net areas.

Some of the data used within this employer purpose can be useful within other employer purposes. The planned occupancy of a space may also be the maximum occupancy of a space. Maximum occupancy levels may be limited due to many factors including building services (heating, cooling and ventilation), room areas and emergency escape restrictions. These limits may have an effect on how spaces can be used in the future, which links into the support for repurposing employer purpose. Maximum occupancy numbers may also have a direct impact on support for business questions, a building may not be able accommodate your planned increase in numbers without major alterations.

Occupancy numbers of spaces tend to be a fundamental building requirement. You need to ensure that each space has the required infrastructure to support the required numbers. By including occupancy numbers in your digital design brief, you can directly and automatically check compliance of the developing design with your requirements.

5: MANAGEMENT OF SECURITY AND SURVEILLANCE

"Information should be required or suppressed to support the management of the security and surveillance of the Facility and neighbouring or adjacent sites in line with the security requirements set out in the EIR." - BS 1192-4

This employer purpose is not intended as a way of scheduling the designed security measures. Unlike other employer purposes, intended to establish what data you want within your model, this employer purpose details the information you should not include within your asset model and project data drops. A data drop is the term that we use to describe the delivery of predefined information at a predefined point during your project. Data drops are defined within your EIR, refer to Chapter 11: Employer's Information Requirements (EIR).

This employer purpose links into *PAS 1192-5:2015 Specification for security-minded building information modelling, digital built environments and smart asset management.*

PAS 1192-5 requires you to assess the security requirements of your facility and neighbouring facilities. The assessment produces a security classification S1-S4. It ranges from S1, the highest security rating where your asset and neighbouring assets are classified as being sensitive, through to S4 where neither your asset or neighbouring assets are considered sensitive. The full definition of a sensitive asset is provided within the guidance, but sensitive assets include government buildings and buildings that have an identified security threat, such as transport hubs and large-capacity sports venues.

It could be a requirement that information is not included within a general data drop if that information could provide a security risk. Access codes and passwords for accessing IP (network) connected assets may not be included within the full set of data, but included within a subset of data that has controlled distribution.

Covert cameras or CCTV data could also be included only within a limited subset of project data. This would ensure that camera locations are restricted to a controlled group, thereby reducing the likelihood that the locations will become common knowledge.

You should not consider information that may be sensitive to your facility in isolation. You also need to consider information that could be sensitive to adjacent facilities. As an example, site survey information will normally contain locations of below-ground services. The surveyed services will not be limited to those directly affecting your facility, but will also include all services in the vicinity of your project. This information may contain valuable information for those wanting to understand data and power supplies to an adjacent building. If this information is linked to your facility model and accessible through hyperlinks, it may become easily accessible. This could then pose a security threat to the sensitive adjacent facility.

6: SUPPORT FOR REPURPOSING

"Repurposing of each Space (location) and the whole Facility should be supported with detailed information about the capacity, in terms of areas, volumes, occupancy, environmental conditions and structural load bearing." - BS 1192-4

This employer purpose also overlaps with others, including support for business questions and management of capacity and utilisation, particularly if you require occupancy data.

When we consider repurposing, we are looking to obtain data that will help with future, as yet unknown, uses for the facility.

Repurposing is not concerned with delivering an estate with future flexibility, as the design will have been developed with this in mind. Buildings that can be adapted for other uses may include, for example, lightweight partitions, services that are contained only within main service runs and heating zones and controls.

The problem with future flexibility is that unless there is actual planned guidance for future uses - for example, the London Aquatics Centre, which was designed for the London 2012 Olympics with spectator seating of 17,500, to be reduced to a sustainable 2,800 after the Olympics - then it's an impossible task to provide a design that caters for every possible option. Education buildings are usually designed to deliver current educational needs. Future educational needs are difficult to accurately predict, due to the influence of government decisions, variable student numbers and changes in demand.

Repurposing by itself doesn't attempt to provide design solutions to this. Instead, it provides design information to assist with understanding the inherent limitations of the facility.

It's easy to see how having easily accessible structural capacity information could help when you are assessing possible new uses for a space. The design of floor slabs will be based upon the type of use for a space, or the building as whole. Different types of uses, such as residential, office, education, or other institutions have different allowable live loads, that is, the combined weight of people or unfixed goods in a building. The design of the building will influence options for a change of use, especially if you are considering a use that will impose higher loads.

Data can also be used for a simple assessment of whether a single space can be changed from a two-person office to a three-person office. Such a change may have restrictions due to the ventilation within the space, the size of the space (you may have your own restrictions on the minimum area per person), or capacity due to escape route restrictions.

7: PREDICTED AND ACTUAL IMPACTS

"The employer should require information relating to the Impacts from cost, carbon (CO2e), energy, waste, water consumption or other environmental effects." - BS 1192-4

The are a couple of ways to consider this purpose. First, the design and the data for a facility can be developed to allow monitoring of impacts. This would mean the design including sufficient metering, submetering and access to data for it to be monitored for anomalies and checked against the loads predicted within the design. But in addition, this purpose could also be used for monitoring embedded carbon and the impact of transport of materials during the delivery phase.

Not all impacts will necessarily be required on all projects. And neither will the predicted and actual impacts necessarily be required for all projects.

As with all the employer purposes, if an employer purpose is required then both the required data (the attributes, parameters and what they are required for) and the stage at which the data is supplied should be clearly identified. You need to be really specific about what you want and when you want it, as this starts to provide you with the details of what you require. We go further into the subject within Chapter 13: Employer's data requirements and BIM data template.

It goes without saying that if your facility requires ongoing monitoring of impacts for items such as energy, waste and water, then appropriate methods for monitoring, recording and distributing the information need to be considered. What type of meters will be used? Will they need to be manually read, or can the data be accessed remotely? What requires metering? Do you require departmental sub-metering? Will you be subletting areas of the building?

If you require embedded carbon information, you need to be clear what you want to measure and how you want that data to be provided. A simpler approach could be to assign the Building Research Establishment (BRE) Green Guide to Specification ratings for products.

If you do this from the start of your project, you can also monitor the embedded carbon as the project develops, as well as the impact of any changes.

It's also possible to add your own information (or parameters). For example if you want to understand the impact of the transport of materials, you could add data for the location of the final manufacture or assembly of materials. This would enable you to compare impacts between projects.

Another way to consider this employer purpose is that it can provide useful benchmarking information. Through it, you can obtain data that will allow objective comparisons throughout the development of your project, throughout the life of your facility and with other facilities. This means trends can be identified that could help you to use your facilities in better ways, or to develop better future facilities.

Consider the following questions: What effects do factors such as outside temperatures, humidity, and wind speed and direction have on energy use? How does this compare between buildings? Does the tested air permeability (sometimes referred to as air tightness) have an effect?

I'm not attempting to tell you what data you should have and what you need to measure, but this should give you some ideas of of the types of data available and how it can be put to use.

If you can provide evidence that a building with low air permeability, provides considerable energy savings compared with a building with higher air permeability, you can start to justify the reason why new projects should aim for buildings that are as airtight as possible.

8: OPERATIONS

"Information necessary for the normal operations of the Facility should be provided to support the facility operators and the employer to anticipate costs of operations." - BS 1192-4

This employer purpose is intended to enable the forecasting of the future costs of a facility, or estate.

Data for this employer purpose should be collected from the earliest stage of your project. It has close links to the support for business questions employer purpose. Not only will the information feed directly into the support for business questions employer purpose, it will also allow you to monitor the design development and understand the long-term costs due to design changes.

The data required for anticipating the costs of operation will be large and varied. Current technology means it won't be practical to include all of the possible data for this employer purpose within your model. However, including some of the relevant data will have benefits and as your design develops the information becomes more reliable as there will be fewer assumptions as actual products are selected.

We can consider four broad areas:

- Energy costs.
- Planned preventative maintenance activities.
- Planned replacement.
- Ongoing facility costs such as management staff, employee costs, rates and consumables.

Due to the diverse nature of the data for the last item, ongoing facility costs, it's unlikely that you will consider using your model as the storage container for this information. That's not to say that you don't add or consider such items. If you require this data to collected, then you should understand what you need, why you need it, where the data will come from and who will have responsibility for that data.

The exact requirements will need to be detailed within your Organisational Information Requirements (OIR), but this data will not be managed through your model. The OIR provides the framework and detail of your full data and information requirements, not just your model data. We will look into the OIR later.

There are clearly other costs in running a facility such as reactive maintenance costs, due to damage or material failures. Due to their unpredictable nature, these cannot be accurately assessed and are probably best added as a contingency, which will be based upon the historical costs of your current facilities. Your data requirements can be included within your OIR for inclusion outside of your project model.

We looked at energy costs within the predicted and actual impacts employer purpose and we will look at planned preventative maintenance and planned replacement within the next two employer purposes. This illustrates how many of the employer purposes are interlinked ... not a problem, as long as your requirements do not conflict and that you are really clear and detailed on the specifics of what you require.

It's also worth noting that the data within the model will not usually contain cost information. But, it will contain detailed information so you can assess the resources and materials required for tasks, or the amount of planned energy required for the facility. This data can then be combined with accurate and current cost data to provide reliable and auditable data for inclusion within your running costs assessments.

9: MAINTENANCE AND REPAIR

"Information on the recommended maintenance tasks, including planned preventative maintenance (PPM), should be provided to support the facility operators to anticipate and plan for costs of maintenance." - BS 1192-4

This takes us back to the very first employer purpose, register. The assets you register are those that can be supplemented with other data, the other employer purposes. In other words, if you require maintenance and repair information for an asset, that asset needs to be registered.

The basic requirement of the maintenance and repair employer purpose is to provide a schedule of tasks. The tasks should provide a comprehensive list of activities required for planned preventative maintenance (PPM) of your assets.

You may not want PPM details for every asset. Therefore, you need to explicitly identify the assets for which you do require such information.

PPM tasks should align with those recommended by the manufacturer or supplier of the asset. Product warranties normally require assets to be maintained in accordance with the manufacturer's recommendations for the warranty to remain valid. Ensuring that product warranties remain valid is particularly important for high-value, mission-critical assets such as air-handling units, and assets that cannot be easily replaced such as cladding and roofing materials. If an asset requires PPM but you don't have the information from the manufacturer then it's probably a safe approach to follow industry best practice and follow guidance as provided by *SFG20 - Standard Maintenance Specification for Building and Engineering Services*.

In this employer purpose, tasks are scheduled as either recurring, which apply to the regular PPM requirements of an asset, or as one-off tasks such as commissioning tasks or planned end-of-life replacement tasks.

For each task it's also possible to provide additional information such as associated risks and the resources required to complete a task. Risks are closely related to health and safety and requirements should be listed within the support for compliance and regulatory responsibilities employer purpose. Whilst resources will link into the operations employer purpose.

10: REPLACEMENT

"Information on the reference or expected replacement service life and costs should be available to the facility operators and to the employer to anticipate the costs of replacement. Recycling of the physical assets should be supported with detailed information relating to the principal constituent materials." - BS 1192-4

We are getting close to the end of the employer purposes, just one more after this one.

As with many of the other employer purposes, the data for the anticipated life of an asset and the cost of replacement is closely related to both the operations and the support for business questions employer purposes.

To accurately forecast the operational cost of a facility, data is required from various sources. The assets that will need replacing within any given period and the cost of replacing those assets should be included in any assessment.

The data for the expected service life and replacement costs is relatively simple, at first glance. Expected service life is a set period of time and the replacement cost of an asset is a numerical monetary value. This alone will provide useful data. However, the replacement cost data needs clarifying, as it could be the direct cost of the asset at the time of installation, or it could be a predicted cost based upon an inflation index compounded over the expected life of the asset. It doesn't matter what method you use, as long as you are consistent and transparent.

Additional data can be added for activities, such as the removal and reinstallation of an asset.

"Recycling of the physical assets should be supported with detailed information relating to the principal constituent materials." - BS 1192-4

By identifying the constituent materials within an asset, the current recycling and disposal requirements can be identified for those materials. As recycling requirements are subject to regular change, this is a more robust approach than associating recycling requirements directly with individual asset types. IFC has another property set *Pset_EnvironmentalImpactValues*, that could provide useful information for the environmental impact of constituent materials.

11: DECOMMISSIONING AND DISPOSAL

"Information on the recommended decommissioning Jobs should be provided to support the facility operators to anticipate and plan for end-of-life costs." - BS 1192-4

Finally, the last of the employer purposes and one of the simplest.

This expands upon the replacement employer purpose. It adds activities and processes for the end of life of the whole facility. Costs can then be associated with the activities. This also links into the support for business questions employer purpose. The assessment of whether a facility is sustainable should also include the costs of decommissioning a facility.

This employer purpose could be used to make sure you have robust information that will allow decommissioning and disposal to take place in the most effective way possible. For example, is your model suitable for calculating the primary materials contained within your facility, such as the volume of concrete or steelwork? This requires that items such as the structure to be modelled in a suitable way. If you look at the structural frame, does the model contain duplicate or overlapping elements? Removing such errors will produce more accurate quantities. This employer purpose also requires all your constituent parts to be classified or named in a consistent way, such as concrete slabs, reinforced foundations and structural steelwork. This means you can ensure that all parts of the structure can be correctly grouped together and scheduled.

Residual risk items relevant to the end-of-life decommissioning such as post-tensioned slabs, which have an inherent risk of sudden failure if the tendons are cut, should also be available for this employer purpose. For some facilities there may be no residual risks relevant to end-of-life decommissioning, whereas other facilities such as laboratories may contain considerable risks and hazards.

EMPLOYER PURPOSES AND YOUR ORGANISATIONAL INFORMATION REQUIREMENTS (OIR)

Employer purposes provide an excellent and accessible approach to understanding your data needs and the uses for your data. All of which is essential for developing a comprehensive OIR. We take a more detailed look at your OIR in Chapter 12: Organisational and Asset Information Requirements (OIR and AIR).

However, your model data and the uses for it will be just one part of your OIR. Not all your OIR will be contained or available through your estate data models.

Establishing employer purposes will go a long way to developing your OIR, it's an important first step. But don't stop there - each project you undertake will help you to refine your process and obtain better, more relevant data.

CHAPTER SUMMARY

One of the most important reasons for having an EIR is so you can set out your exact data requirements.

Employer purposes provide focus on the reason why you are obtaining data. You have a specific need and you obtain data to fulfill your need.... Data has a cost, obtaining data from your supply chain will have a cost and maintaining your data will have a cost.

- Establish your data requirements using the BS 1192-4 framework, referred to as employer purposes.

- The BS 1192-4 employer purposes:
    - Register
    - Support for business questions
    - Support for compliance and regulatory responsibilities
    - Management of capacity and utilisation
    - Management of security and surveillance
    - Support for repurposing
    - Predicted and actual impacts
    - Operations
    - Maintenance and repair
    - Replacement
    - Decommissioning and disposal

- Your employer purposes should form part of your OIR, your OIR informs your EIR.

CHAPTER 6: MODEL CHECKING

Check - *Examine (something) in order to determine its accuracy, quality, or condition, or to detect the presence of something.*
Check something against - *Verify the accuracy of something by comparing it with (something else).* (Oxford Dictionaries)

WHAT IS MODEL CHECKING?

Design has evolved over millennia, with 2D design being the norm for around 4,000 years.

It is now increasingly common for designers, including architects, structural engineers, building services engineers and even landscape architects to develop and present their designs as digital 3D models. This makes a lot of sense considering the world we live within is in effect a 3D environment, making designs a lot more understandable and easier to envision for clients and end users of a facility.

By combining and overlapping each designer's 3D model, we are able to check for clashes between the designed elements, spot hazardous building scenarios and establish residual risks associated with the ongoing maintenance of the facility, to name but a few. This practice is known as model checking.

Model checking also provides you with the reassurance that your model meets your requirements, as detailed within your Employer's Information Requirements (EIR).

WHY MODEL CHECK?

Building on Chapter 2 - BIM as the container for your building data, in which I identified the importance of an EIR and Chapter 4 - Establishing your organisational data, where I looked at the importance of providing your exact data requirements, you can begin to see why you need a comprehensive EIR. There is much more detail on this in Chapter 11 - Employer's Information Requirements (EIR).

An EIR tells you exactly what data is required within the project model, when it is required and who is responsible for delivering this information.

But how do you know that you have the information you have requested?

You can take a passive approach and rely on those delivering the information to validate or confirm that it is correct. Of course, the professional team delivering your project for you should be delivering the correct information. However, this is clearly a risky approach. You wouldn't normally accept something of considerable value without doing some checks yourself.

The alternative is to take an active approach: to check the model yourself or obtain an independent check.

WHAT IS THE MODEL CHECKED AGAINST?

It's easy to establish the benchmark - or what the model will be checked against - for model data. It will be checked against your EIR deliverables.

This highlights the importance of developing an EIR with clear deliverables, with the added benefits that it will:

    A. Enable your professional team to plan for the provision of your deliverables.

    B. Clarify your requirements.

    C. Make it easy for you to check your requirements have been met.

Model checking enables you to verify that your model aligns with the requirements of your EIR.

It enables you to use your model for the purposes you have defined for it, whether that's obtaining model quantities, visualizations, facilities management data or the other model uses available to you.

DATA AND QUALITY

Model checking should cover the data and the quality of the graphical elements of the model.

The model data is often more valuable than than the graphical 3D model itself, although in a good model, they should go hand-in-hand. The graphical objects need to be accurately located and represented within the 3D model so that the associated data is useful. For example, you have to be sure that when data is associated with a fire damper, that the fire damper is located in the correct location, the actual location where it has been installed, for the data to be meaningful. Data about a fire damper has limited use if you can't locate the damper, resulting in little more than a traditional asset list.

The graphical model data will also become useful for future redesign and repurposing of spaces or a whole facility.

TYPES OF MODEL CHECKS

There are various types of checks that you can do. Ideally, for transparency and to promote collaboration, your project professionals who are responsible for delivering graphical and data models should be fully aware of the types of checks you will do and the detail you will be checking. This also promotes accountability by making everyone aware of what you require and what you will be checking.

All models should be checked by the originator of the model before they are shared with other organisations. Each organisation should check its models meet the requirements of the EIR, that the data has been validated and the the model meets the quality requirements.

Model checks can be categorised into two groups: non-graphical pure data checks; and graphical model quality data checks.

NON-GRAPHICAL PURE DATA CHECKS

Non-graphical data checks are objective. They are binary. Either the data has been provided or it hasn't.

At this stage, you are comparing whether or not the data has been provided in line with your EIR. If your EIR doesn't explicitly detail your data requirements, the parameters that you require for each type of component, the organisation responsible for providing the data and at what stage the information should be provided, then you don't have anything to measure against. Without this, your data check would become a subjective assessment. You would be checking that your professional team had guessed and provided the data that you want, but that you haven't detailed.

The data checks can also be used to assess the quality of the data provided. This becomes more of an objective approach. If you ask for the manufacturer's name to be provided for each maintainable asset, then there are only limited automated checks that can be done.

You can check that the entered text does not contain any unusual characters (such as *, %, or $), you can check that the text does not contain an unusual amount of numerical characters and that the length of the text provided is within reasonable bounds.

You can also provide other restrictions on the information allowed, for example, you could make sure the input for a date field will only accept a date, or that a numerical field will only accept numbers.

This is where humans can supplement the data validation. It's always useful to do your own visual scan of the data provided. You can do this by, for example, producing a schedule of all manufacturers and scanning down the names to see if anything stands out as being odd. This won't be foolproof, but in addition to the automated data checks, it will allow you to have a high level of confidence in your data, specifically your non-graphical data.

Finally, your model data can be assessed against your specific requirements for the proposed asset. The checks can include the areas of spaces and zones are this in accordance with your requirements. They also include performance criteria such as designed occupancy, maximum and minimum temperatures and acoustics. One way of checking this is by assessing against a digital design brief.

GRAPHICAL MODEL QUALITY CHECKS

The graphical elements of your model are the things you can see when you view your model, using a suitable application.

You can if you really want, although I wouldn't recommend this, view your IFC model in the raw text file format. This contains all the graphical and non-graphical elements in a data-only format.

Returning back to viewing your graphical model. The quality of your graphical model tells you how well the model has been put together. It provides an assessment of the coordination of all the model objects - whether the objects fit together properly in a logical way.

It also provides an assessment of the model design in accordance with statutory, and your own, design requirements. For example, one of your requirements may be that electrical distribution boards are not located within occupied spaces, and a statutory requirement would include the floor area for accessible toilets.

Finally, graphical checks assess the detail of the objects. This is referred to as level of detail (LOD).

GRAPHICAL COORDINATION CHECKS

Graphical coordination checks monitor how the objects fit and work together. They can also put categories into different types of checks, such as clash detection, proximity checks and compliance checks.

Clash detection: This is the simplest type of coordination check. A clash occurs when two or more objects occupy the same space. It's a bit like having a door within a wall without having an opening within the wall. There are also some less obvious clashes, such as duplicates when two identical objects existing in the same space and overlapping objects of the same type.

Overlapping objects often occur within walls and floor slabs. Overlapping and duplicate objects wouldn't cause much of a problem if the model was only used for providing drawings and details at the design and construction phase. But, if you want to use your model for any other purposes, then duplicates and overlapping components should be removed.

Tools that identify clash detection within a model include Autodesk Navisworks, Solibri Model Checker and the free Tekla BIMsight.

Proximity checks: These are a couple of steps along in terms of complexity. Proximity checks identify whether one type of object is too close to another type of object. The objects that are being checked will not directly clash or exist within the same space, as those issues will be picked up through clash detection.

A typical proximity issue occurs when a column is located too close to a door or a window. The column does not clash, but it shouldn't be located close to a door to restrict access or to restrict the swing of a door.

A column also shouldn't be located in front of a window, preventing access and reducing light.

For proximity checks to work, the checking application needs to understand what objects are. An application will need to know (or assess) that a door is a door and column is a column. It may seem odd that a checking application wouldn't know that a door is a door, or that a column is a column. We can view graphical objects within the 3D model and our knowledge enables us to understand, or at least make a good guess, of what the objects are representing. Applications do not have this level of intelligence, they need to either be explicitly informed of what the objects are or use simplistic logic to categorise the objects.

The data to identify or categorise objects is added to each object. Once objects are categorised, you can then check the relative location of different types of objects.

The proximity checks use simple, logical rules. Proximity checks are specific to combinations of objects and specify a required clearance measurement. For a window, you could check that there is sufficient clearance to the plane of a window from objects such as pipes, columns, doors and fixed furniture. With the acceptable clearance information, the model is checked and issues are raised when objects are located inside the clearance zone.

Compliance checks: The final type of check is for compliance of the design with specific requirements. These could be approved documents, BREEAM, British Standards or project-specific design requirements.

For example, accessible WCs require a certain floor area and specific fixtures in particular locations. Platform lifts require a minimum floor area to the entrances. There are countless other potential model compliance checks.

> *Adding new logical compliance checks should be an ongoing process and part of your normal workflow.*

Each time you come across an issue or problem, always look at it in a logical way. Think about whether you can develop a logical check that would provide an early warning for an issue that may arise. As an example, a single-ply roof requires a minimum 150mm upstand around the perimeter of the roof finish, so that the single-ply can be turned up, fixed to the upstand and a trim applied over it. Without this minimum upstand, single-ply manufacturer and installers can not provide a warranty for the installation. Yet, it's amazingly common how often the minimum 150mm upstand is not provided throughout the full perimeter of a roof finish. This type of check is easy to implement, it identifies any potential problems early in the design process, allowing simple design fixes before they become costly issues.

Developing logical checks could be an outcome of lessons learnt workshops. Or they could be developed through a workshop at the start of a project, where all stakeholders get together to pool their collective knowledge and assess what may go wrong. Logical checks will never be a panacea for preventing all problems from occurring, some issues will not be suitable for converting into logical checks and new problems will always arise.

But, in time, your library of logical checks will become a valuable resource that will enable you to reduce risks.

LEVEL OF DETAIL (LOD) AND LEVEL OF INFORMATION (LOI)

Level of detail (LOD) and level of information (LOI) tell you how much detail or information is required within a model.

We define the LOD and LOI required at specific stages during the design and construction stages of a project. We normally use the RIBA stages, or similar, from stages 0 through to stage 7 (in use).

> *LOD describes the detail or the complexity of the graphical contents of a model.*

A simple way to understand LOD is to consider how an everyday office chair can be graphically represented within a model. At its simplest, a chair could be represented as a box or a three-dimensional cuboid, with overall dimensions similar to those of the chair. However, if you looked at this object within a model, you wouldn't get any visual cues as to what it was. But, comprehensive data could be added to this object to provide detailed non-graphical information. Graphical detail and the amount of non-graphical data are not linked. As long as you have a simple cuboid, you can add all the information required. Similarly, you could have a model that was fully accurate in every way to the real object, but with minimal non-graphical data.

LOD 2 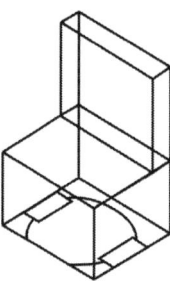 LOD 3  LOD 4

As the level of detail increases, the chair begins to represent the shape of a chair, perhaps as a couple of cuboids arranged to look like a simple chair to begin with. At the next level of detail you could have a model object that provides a detailed representation of a chair. Finally, at the highest level of detail, the graphical chair would accurately depict the actual chair within your facility.

During the early days of BIM in the UK, until around 2013, we only had LOD. At the time it was thought that the LOD of the model was sufficient. As such, in the CIC BIM Protocol's first edition (2013), the Appendix 1 Model Production and Development Table references LOD but has no mention of LOI. Although PAS 1192-2, published the same year referenced LOI.

It's important to understand that LOD and LOI are two different things. They describe different aspects of a model and, as we looked at earlier, they do not have to be the same.

Because the LOD reference and the LOI reference at a defined stage during design do not have to be the same, it became essential that they were separated so they could be measured independently.

The PAS 1192-2 Specification for information management for the capital/delivery phase of construction projects using building information modelling references and provides clarity around LOD and LOI. The specification also combines them into a new term - Levels of Model Definition (LOMD).

The LOMD definition from *PAS 1192-3* includes the phrases "minimum level of detail needed by the team or the employer for each model's purposes shall be defined" and "the level of graphical information and data to be delivered at each information exchange". It also provides tables that help with defining the required LOMD.

This means that when we refer to the general model detail as a combination of both graphical and non-graphical information, we should use the term LOMD.

But when we are specifically referring to only the graphical data, we use the term LOD, and when we are referring to only the associated, non-graphical data, we use the term LOI.

NBS BIM TOOLKIT DEFINITIONS

In the UK, we have the NBS BIM toolkit to help us define LOD (and also LOI, but more on that later). The NBS BIM toolkit provides a series of web pages that align with the Uniclass 2015 codes that are also managed and developed by the NBS. This means that you can look up the Uniclass Product code for doorset systems *Ss_25_30_20_25* and see a graphical representation, with descriptions, of how a doorset system will look as the detail increases from LOD 2 through to LOD 5. It's a great resource when attempting to define your requirements within your EIR.

There are a couple of points to note about the NBS LOD definitions. The first is that not all the Uniclass codes have an LOD definition page, which is understandable as the product Pr table alone has more than 6,000 codes. I would hope that, over time, the available definitions will be enhanced. The second is that some of the definitions are generic, indeed the same definition is used for multiple codes, which again is understandable with the high number of codes and given that some are quite similar.

There is also a shortcut you can use to directly access a definition.

The first step is to access any LOD definition. If you look into the address bar of your web browser, you can see that the address ends with the Uniclass code that you have accessed.

For the above doorset system, the web address is:

>   *https://toolkit.thenbs.com/Definitions/Ss_25_30_20_25/*

By changing the Uniclass code at the end of the web address to another Uniclass code, you can directly access another definition.

This provides the information and background behind LOD, but LOI should be treated in a different way.

My approach to LOI has changed since I started my BIM journey. I initially treated LOI in a similar way to LOD. This approach was supported by the NBS definitions. The NBS definition that provides commentary and typical images for LOD also contains similar information for LOI. However, I no longer refer to the NBS toolkit for LOI.

Let me explain why I have taken this approach.

The NBS toolkit generic type approach works reasonably well for LOD (although, not perfectly) and it was the place where I started when understanding LOI. LOD works reasonably well because we are used to seeing design information, in the way of 2D drawings, that looks different when created by different designers. Therefore, as long as the graphical design somehow aligns with the descriptions and images within the NBS toolkit, we can be satisfied that the required LOD has been reached. However, data is all together different.

> For data to be useful, it cannot almost align with a generic requirement, it needs to exactly align with a very specific requirement. This doesn't mean that we drop LOI, it just means that instead of providing a general description of what an LOI should look like, we provide exact requirements. At BIMsense, we detail the exact data that is required for each data drop or information exchange.

The data should be specific to the needs of your project, it should include all the data that you require and exclude the data that you do not require.

At BIMsense, our EIRs include the exact detail of which IFC entities require data, the data attributes required for each entity and when the information is provided (which usually aligns with the data drops, or information exchanges.

So an EIR with detailed data requirements fulfils the same role as LOI, it avoids any of the generalities associated with the NBS BIM Toolkit LOI. It also enables us to objectively validate the non-graphical data. It makes it simple to assess whether the data has been provided. It provides an unambiguous yes or no answer.

Conversely, this does mean that validation of LOD is currently subjective and open to ambiguity. But, the visual approach of validating graphical components works for the time being. Although, I'm convinced that this will also change, and at some point we will be able to objectively assess if objects meet the required LOD.

MODEL CHECK RESULTS

The results from model checking need to be collated in a simple format.

Model checks can be compiled into a traditional report format or developed into a spreadsheet schedule. These are traditional approaches that have worked well in the past with paper-based systems.

One benefit of BIM is that it opens the way for new improved and more efficient methods of working. The management of issues and model check results is definitely one of these areas.

We have a new format specifically developed for model check results. An individual model check result identifies a problem, or issue, that requires a resolution. The BIM Collaboration Format (BCF) allows issues to be collected together and managed efficiently, but also introduces new functionalities.

The first point to mention about BCF is that it is designed for collaboration - the clue really is in the name. It does this by adding a unique identifier, called a Globally Unique Identifier (GUID) to every raised issue. It is very unlikely that GUIDs will ever be duplicated, so unlikely in fact that we shouldn't even concern ourselves with the possibility of ever coming across two identical random GUIDs. The unique identifier enables each issue (or each BCF) to be shared and commented on by multiple stakeholders. When BCFs are merged back together, all the comments relating to a single issue are also combined together.

A BCF also contains other data to assist with collaboration. An image or a snapshot of the issue as viewed within the model can be manually or, most often, automatically added to the BCF. The image provides a permanent record of the issue when viewed. This is useful as the issue when viewed will change as your model is amended. A permanent record of the viewed issue means you can simply assess the effect of these changes by viewing the updated model and comparing it with the image of the original issue. If the updates to the model resolve the problem, the BCF that contains the issue can be closed.

TITLE	Column located in front of window
STATUS	ERROR OPEN
DESCRIPTION	Column C7, is located within 500mm of window W10.
MODEL VIEW	
ADD COMMENT	SEND

USER	POSTED	STATUS	COMMENT
ian.yeo@bimsense.co.uk	1 day ago	Error	Coordination workshop arranged
ian.yeo@bimsense.co.uk	5 days ago	Error	Issue remains unresolved
ian.yeo@bimsense.co.uk	10 days ago	Error	Issue first identified

The BCF also contains information about the location of the issue. This includes the location of the objects affected by the problem that requires resolution, but also embeds technical information about about how the issue should be viewed.

This means that when using applications such as Autodesk's Revit, with a suitable plugin, you can see the BCF as viewed by the originator.

This not only saves time, as it prevents team members from having to locate a space and then attempt to work out where within the space the issue occurred, it also provides useful information about the issue. You all see the issue in exactly the same view, as the originator intended, which provides useful insights into the issue.

THE ECONOMICS OF MODEL CHECKING

At BIMsense we are often asked to justify the additional costs associated with model checking.

It's difficult for businesses to approve spending, especially when this additional expense was not required on previous projects. All businesses should take effective action to reduce risks and model checking undoubtedly reduces risks. However, justification of costs is often a necessary barrier to cross.

We aggregate all our model checking data and provide our clients with an assessment of the benefits and likely cost savings of checking your models.

The findings from this data show that for each model check, the return of investment (ROI) is at least 17x. For each £100 invested in a model check, the project will save £1700 due to the early elimination of issues.

The calculation takes into account the average number of issues and critical issues identified compared with the value of the project. Over time we will continue to improve our data to provide ROI information for specific building types, sectors and project stages.

The ROI also increases as the value of the project increases. For projects of around £3 million the ROI is 17x, but for projects in excess of £30 million we get a 25x ROI.

The design team needs to work collaboratively to close out and resolve the issue identified through the model checking. Subsequent and follow-up model checks for the same project will result in a gradually lower ROI.

> It's clear that model checking not only benefits a project by reducing overall risks it also has an identified benefit by saving costs.

If I was directly involved in managing a project I really wouldn't be able to justify not checking the quality of project models.

CHAPTER SUMMARY

Model checking allows you to verify that your model aligns with the requirements of your EIR. It enables you to use your model for the purposes you have defined for it.

- Model checking can be separated into two distinct types:

    - Checking the visual elements of the model, the way the parts of a model fit together (coordination checks) and how much detail is contained within the model.

    - Checking the non-visual elements, the data contained within your model, what data has been provided and that it is correct.

- Your model checks should be clear and transparent in terms of what will be checked and how the checks will be validated (what is and is not acceptable). This information should be included within your EIR.

- Who does the checking is an important consideration, will you want the benefits of independently validate your designers' models?

- Model checking will significantly reduce your exposure to risks by ensuring the design meets your requirements and is free from errors.

CHAPTER 7: BIM COMPETENCY

Competency - *The ability to do something successfully or efficiently.* (Oxford English Dictionary)

THE IMPORTANCE OF COMPETENCY

It may be obvious, but it's worth saying that it's important for any project to have involvement from competent people and organisations. Not only will this reduce a significant number of project risks, it will enable the project to proceed in an efficient and organised manner.

You need to make sure that the organisations involved in your project are able to do exactly what is required of them (or, in some circumstances, that they have a plan in place to develop their competency to deliver your requirements).

When it comes to design that impacts upon health and safety, the Construction (Design and Management) or CDM Regulations 2015 issued by the UK Health and Safety Executive, make it a legal requirement for organisations who provide any sort of design to be assessed for competency.

> *If BIM is a deliverable requirement for your project, you need to be sure that the organisations you employ are competent to deliver your BIM requirements.*

And, of course, the assessment of competency needs to take place during the procurement or appointment process. It's very disruptive to find out, deep into your project, that an important member of your team is unable to deliver a key requirement.

ASSESSING BIM COMPETENCY

Competency is relatively easy to assess for most of your project requirements, using established methods. For individuals, you have competency assessment cards, such as the Construction Skills Certification Scheme (CSCS) - which provide proof that individuals working on construction sites have the required training and qualifications - and you have membership of established professional bodies. And for organisations, there are certifications and accreditations that confirm compliance with standards, trade bodies and independent assessment bodies.

But how do you assess competency in the new area of BIM, at a time when BIM requirements are not yet mature enough to follow the above methods?

In this chapter, I will look in detail at ways you can assess BIM competency.

However, you may not feel confident enough in your own BIM competency to assess the competency of other organisations. This is completely understandable. If you find yourself in this position, the best approach is engage with a trusted BIM consultancy such as BIMsense, who can either advise you or provide you with an impartial assessment of the BIM competency of your proposed supply chain.

It is also worth noting that being BIM competent is subjective. One person's perception of what it takes to become a BIM specialist will not be the same as someone else's. During procurement, such claims should be investigated so that you are satisfied that marketing or tender-response content is indeed a true reflection of practical experience or certification status. I touch on this in more detail later in this chapter.

Ultimately, when assessing BIM competency, you want to be sure that all the organisations involved in your project can deliver your specific BIM requirements, and not generic requirements that are not applicable to you.

BIM CERTIFICATION

We are now beginning to see the emergence of BIM certifications, which align with the requirements of the current guidance documents *PAS 1192-2* and *PAS 1192-3*. For a fee, organisations such as the BSI, BRE and Stroma will assess an organisation for compliance with the current standards, and provide certification if that organisation's BIM procedures align with the PAS standards.

However, the UK does not currently have a professional body to actively oversee and monitor certificate providers. The United Kingdom Accreditation Service (UKAS) has been tasked by UK government to accredit the organisations that offer certifications, but the process remains ongoing. The most recent update from UKAS was in June 2017, but didn't provide a timetable for implementation.

> *If an organisation has a certificate for compliance with the requirements of PAS 1192-2, then this is a really good indication that it will be able to deliver your BIM requirements.*

We are primarily concerned here with competency to *PAS 1192-2*, compliance with the standard for BIM during the design and construction phase of a project. Compliance with *PAS 1192-3*, BIM standards for the occupancy of a facility, would be less useful for a delivery organisation, although it should be a goal for all organisations with a large estate.

That said, I don't think you should rely solely on a certificate of compliance. Practical experience aligned to your needs should also be considered, which I take a closer look at later in this chapter.

There are also some specific details of certification that may come as a surprise. A certificate of compliance is specific to a single company. So if you have an organisation that has regional offices, each of which is organised as an individual company, a limited company or a limited liability partnership, each will require certification. This also applies to an organisation at the head of a group of companies - the company at group level may be certified but the individual companies that make up that group may not be. It's important to have a copy of the certificate, which should provide details of the extent and limits of the certification. If you are at all unsure, contact the organisation that issued the certificate.

In some ways, the initial assessment and certification can be slightly easier than they are in subsequent years. This is because when the initial assessment takes place, any areas of minor non-compliance are identified for rectification by the next annual assessment. For this reason, always check that the certificate is up to date.

With the current limited availability of organisations that have BIM certification, you also need other methods to assess competency. Here, I look at four alternative methods of assessing competency: standard BIM assessment forms; experience; pre-contract BIM Execution Plans; and previous project models.

STANDARD BIM ASSESSMENT FORMS

There are a couple of widely available BIM competency assessments. The most widely used and referenced assessment is the CPIx BIM Assessment Form. The CPIx forms have gained a high level of credibility because they are directly referenced within *PAS 1192-2*. However, the CPIx forms date back to 2011. The industry, our understanding of BIM and our requirements have all moved on in that time.

I wouldn't suggest that you use the CPIx assessment forms. By all means take a look at the forms and see if there is anything that could be useful to you. But in my experience, answering a question such as "What is your definition of collaboration?" is too subjective and providing evidence of your understanding of the "12 Areas of BIM" will not help you to assess whether an organisation is competent. At worst these forms will require an organisation to do unnecessary work in answering the questions, and at best you will receive a generic response.

You could develop your own organisation-specific BIM assessment, with relevant and useful questions. This could be a useful tool and greatly assist in assessing the quality of your potential suppliers.

In the future, we may see a widely accepted register of organisations with relevant BIM competency, something similar to Constructionline (for construction suppliers) or CHAS (for construction health and safety competency).

PAS 91, the pre-qualification questionnaire, has a reasonably good section specific to BIM. It allows organisations with certification to pass the section without requiring further information and permits the use of supporting evidence for those without certification. Table 8 of PAS 91 provides four concise questions, with supporting information, which in my opinion, provide a better starting point for developing competency questions than those contained in the CPIx BIM Assessment Form.

The four questions are:

1. Do you have the capability of working with a project using a Common Data Environment as described in PAS 1192-2 : 2013?

2. Do you have documented policy, systems and procedures to achieve Level 2 BIM maturity as defined in the government's BIM strategy?

3. Do you have the capability of developing and delivering or working to....a BIM Execution Plan (BEP) as described in PAS 1192-2 : 2013?

4. Do you have arrangements for training employees in BIM-related skills and do you assess their capabilities?

BIM EXPERIENCE

An organisation's BIM experience can be a really good starting point to assess competency. But, the experience you use as evidence needs to be relevant to your requirements.

It will be of little relevance to appoint an organisation that can produce photorealistic visuals from the project model, but can't deliver the project requirement of a data-rich model.

If you make sure your project Employer's Information Requirements (EIR) are available at the earliest stages of a project, even if there are incomplete sections, organisations will be able to understand the specific BIM requirements of your project and (hopefully) provide only relevant experience.

BIM EXECUTION PLANS (BEPS)

A BIM Execution Plan (BEP) is an essential part of a successful BIM project, it enables everyone to be clear on exactly what they need to do to deliver collaborative BIM. It considers the project BIM requirements from the EIR and details how the requirements will be delivered.

Put simply, an EIR confirms your wants and needs in terms of BIM deliverables. The BEP is your supplier's response to the EIR, confirming their interpretation of your expectations and how they propose to deliver them, it provides the framework for your design and delivery team to deliver your project's BIM requirements.

A BEP takes into account the organisations involved in the project, the systems, the data deliverables, the stage deliverables, the common data environment and any other BIM-relevant factors. It pulls all the information into a plan for delivery and responsibilities, it's shared with the whole project team and is updated throughout the project.

The BEP should be bespoke to your project. It should directly respond to your Employer's Information Requirements (EIR), which is covered in detail in Chapter 11, and it should provide clear detail on how your specific requirements will be delivered.

It may be that a supplier's BEP is not exactly aligned with the client's expectations. Each BEP should be reviewed with variations in mind and judged on the overall benefit and value to the client, and to project requirements.

The requirement for a BIM project to have a BEP is a central part of *PAS 1192-2*.

But, *PAS 1192-2* also requires a pre-contract BIM Execution Plan, which schedules the information that should be contained within the pre-contract BEP.

The pre-contract BEP will not have all the information required for the BEP produced after your designers or contractors are appointed, but it will contain useful information for assessing competency.

This means that your tender responses from your key suppliers, your primary designers and your main contractor, should all include a pre-contract BEP. You should make this requirement crystal clear in your tender documentation. You should also state that the pre-contract BEP should be bespoke for your project. Tender returns often only include an organisation's generic BEP, which may have some use, such as allowing you to see the quality of the document. But a pre-tender BEP tailored for your project will provide a method to assess BIM competency. It also means that the project will have a good starting point as some of the BIM groundwork will already have taken place.

When you assess the pre-contract BEP, you should be checking that it contains the sections as detailed within *PAS 1192-2* and that the information contained is understandable and unambiguous. The dates and responsibilities should align with your project requirements. But, most important is that the pre-contract BEP provides details of how your EIR deliverables will be achieved. This should include any tools and platforms that will be used to do this, including verification of the model and the data contained within the model.

Another good indication of BIM competence is the proposed approach to developing your specific data requirement. Who will have the overall responsibility for the data (this is normally the project information manager)? Who will be responsible for adding data to the model (this could be the lead designer or a data manager)? And how will data be coordinated from the supply chain, which will include specialist designers and subcontractors with design responsibilities? These are all important parts of the data process that will require careful management.

The book does not contain detailed information on how to develop a BEP. As a client, it's very unlikely that you will be required to develop a project BEP. Your main objective is to ensure that your project team is equipped to deliver BIM and one way of doing this is by reviewing and monitoring the design and delivery team BEPs, both the pre-contract BEP and the later post-contract BEP developed after the appointment of your design team and then after the appointment of your contractor.

EXAMPLE BIM MODEL

The final method of assessing BIM competency is by assessing a model. This could be a sample model, which contains the data in the format and for typical objects as detailed in your EIR. Such a sample model would provide a deep understanding of your BIM data requirements and would give you a high degree of confidence in your supplier's BIM competency.

Alternatively, or possibly in addition, you could be provided with access to a model from a previous project. Ideally, this would contain data in a similar format to what you require. Access to a live or recently completed model, in addition to a review of the data, would also allow you to assess the graphical quality of the model.

There may be concerns over intellectual property rights or confidentiality of data. However, you may be able to receive temporary, controlled access to a previous project model through a suitable model viewing application. In this instance, it would be a straightforward process to interrogate some of the most recent model issues and check the data attributes for a sample of objects.

BIM WASH

Don't just take someone's word as evidence of competency. There are a lot of well-intentioned people doing some really great and innovative things with BIM. The problem is that BIM covers an extremely wide spectrum of design, construction and operations. We also all have different interpretations of what BIM competency should look like.

This isn't that I have a general lack of trust in people, quite the opposite. I believe that most people do not want to mislead anyone when it comes to their competency. What long-term benefits can be gained by telling someone you are able to do something that you actually can not? The truth will out at some point and then reputation and trust will be lost. However, we all interpret our abilities and our competencies differently.

BIM wash is a term that has been coined to describe people who talk a good game about what they have achieved. It's where a BIM competency claim is greater than the actual BIM competency of a person or organisation:

BIM Wash = BIM Claim > BIM Competency

It could describe those who intentionally want to mislead. However, as I have said, I don't believe that most people set out to intentionally mislead.

I prefer to think of BIM wash as a difference of interpretations. It's easy for two people to have different interpretations on the BIM Level 2 deliverables. This is completely understandable. A common misconception is that if you have a common data environment, known as a CDE, you are now doing BIM Level 2. A common data environment is an essential part of BIM Level 2, but it is just one piece of the BIM Level 2 requirements.

We need to do all we can to avoid these differences in opinion. Whether you're looking at your data requirements, your deliverables or your BIM competency, make your requirements as explicit as possible.

OUTCOMES OF INSUFFICIENT COMPETENCY

How could we have got to a situation where we have appointed an organisation with insufficient competency? There's little benefit in criticising individuals or organisations for getting into such a position. It could have been due to a project progressing before you became aware of the importance of competency. Or there may have been a general insufficient level of competency within the available supply chain. Whatever the reason, what can you do to get the best possible outcome if you continue on the current course?

What normally happens is that you will have a mixture of organisations, with sufficient and insufficient competency.

The key thing is that your primary designers of architectural, structural and building services and your main contractor have sufficient competency. This will increase your likelihood of achieving a successful BIM project. Your main suppliers will be able to increase competency in the rest of your supply chain, as it will be in their interests to have a successful project.

If the balance is the other way and you have a key supplier (often referred to as a tier 1 supplier) lacking in competency, then it's very unlikely that you will obtain your BIM deliverables without some sort of intervention. The exception here is with your structural designer. In some circumstances, you could obtain BIM deliverables without a BIM-competent structural designer. But do not depend on these unlikely circumstances.

BIM depends on collaboration between your suppliers. Without the necessary BIM competency the collaboration will not be complete. If you had a BIM-competent architect but your building services designer does not have the required competency, then not only will you be missing important building services data, but your architectural model is unlikely to be coordinated.

It's really difficult to fully coordinate a design without the 3D models.

Coordination using 2D information takes an immense amount of resource and only looks at 2D sections of a model, as opposed to the entire model. This means you will not have a high-quality model with high quality and a significant quantity of important data will be missing. It's still possible that you could get some short-term benefits, by having a model that you can test and learn from. But long-term, you will not have trust in your model. You need to have trust and confidence in your model so you can maximise its use for the long term and across your organisation.

INSUFFICIENT COMPETENCY INTERVENTIONS

You realise that one of your appointed key tier 1 suppliers does not have the required level of competency ... what can you do about it and how can you obtain good outcomes?

First, you need to identify insufficient competency as soon as possible and you need your key supplier to accept that they don't have the required level of competency. Regular communication, quality checking and verification will make sure any major problems can be identified before they progress too far. The sooner you can identify problems, the easier they are to fix them.

Second, you should work out mitigation measures. This needs to take place with the agreement of the failing supplier and ideally also with your other key suppliers. Any failings from your key suppliers will inevitably have knock-on effects to your other suppliers, and you need to have your whole team on board to fix the problems. Mitigation measures will be unique to your project, to solve your particular problem.

They could involve: support from an external organisation with the required expertise; training, additional responsibilities for your remaining suppliers; or direct support from you.

You may also need to reconsider your BIM deliverables. Is there anything that is desired, but not absolutely essential? Removing some of your deliverables takes some of the pressure off your suppliers.

CONTRACTUAL BIM

Assuming that you have all the necessary evidence of project-specific competency, you still need to make sure your BIM deliverables are included in your appointment and contract documents. This includes making sure your team is fully aware of its contractual duties and each organisation's specific BIM deliverables.

I can provide some information on this, but it's essential that you seek professional legal advice.

The current advice is that the CIC BIM Protocol is added to existing contract documents, such as NEC3 or JCT, as a set of add-on clauses. The protocol identifies the Building Information Models required to be produced by members of the project team, and puts in place specific obligations, liabilities and associated limitations on the use of the models. The protocol requires you to clearly define your BIM deliverables, either by directly including or referencing your EIR.

However, I have been advised that the protocol conflicts with existing JCT and NEC3 contract clauses. Having ambiguity between your contract documents is never a good thing and could lead to disputes. This is why it is essential to obtain legal advice, in case amendments to the protocol are required to remove any ambiguities with your main contract documents.

INFORMATION MANAGER

The CIC BIM Protocol also requires the appointment of an information manager for your project. This could be the same person as your organisational Information Manager, refer to Chapter 10, or could be an external appointment. The CIC has a complementary publication Outline Scope of Services for the role of Information Management, which aligns an appointment with the protocol.

A project information manager ensures that project BIM procedures as defined within your EIR and your supplier's BEP are followed and that information provided satisfies your BIM deliverables.

The role of information manager, as defined within the *CIC Scope of Services for the role of Information Management* can also include the setting up of a common data environment (CDE), in addition to the management of the CDE.

The CIC Scope of Services for the role of Information Management also identifies that an information manager is not a BIM co-ordinator and has no design responsibility and no responsibility for clash detection or model coordination.

AN EXAMPLE OF A BIM DISPUTE

In May 2016, the Ministry of Defence employed Trant Engineering Ltd to develop and deliver the *Mid-Atlantic Power Project* at the Mount Pleasant Complex in the Falkland Islands. In order to help facilitate the £55m power generation facility, Trant engaged the help of Mott MacDonald to provide design consultancy services including preliminary design, detailed design, design coordination, preparation and implementation of BIM and procurement support, principal designer responsibilities and the development of the DREAM assessment (an environment assessment throughout the design stage).

We won't go into great deal here about the outcome, but the relationship quickly soured and resulted in the earliest recorded BIM-centred UK court case: Trant Engineering Limited v Mott MacDonald Limited, details of which can be easily accessed via an internet search. In summary, measures were taken by Mott MacDonald to supply a proposed contract to Trant outlining its payment terms and scope of services; crucially, explaining the use of their preferred CDE and the access rights within to BIM information for their client, Trant.

Trant did not respond to this proposed contract, nor did it sign and return the contract. Trant did however (as judged by the court) in effect agree to the contract by beginning to pay Mott MacDonald as per the proposed contract terms.

However, following subsequent non-payment of submitted invoices to Trant, Mott MacDonald made the decision to restrict access to BIM data held on the CDE, a clear violation of Mott MacDonald's own contract terms, which allowed full access at all times.

In essence, this case is a reflection of the age-old argument about payments between contractors and subcontractors, but it also highlights the importance of having your BIM contract requirements clearly described in case of a breakdown in relations.

With Trant unable to access BIM information, the primary client, the Ministry of Defence, was disadvantaged by not being able to access information on its project. This case provides a reminder that you should ensure that access to and ownership of your BIM information is clearly defined in the EIR and in pre- and post-contract BEPs, and that these requirements are included in your contract documents.

CHAPTER SUMMARY

If BIM is a deliverable requirement for your project, you need to be sure that the organisations you employ are competent to deliver your BIM requirements.

- BIM competency should be assessed against your specific BIM requirements - your BIM deliverables as detailed within your EIR.

    - Methods of assessing BIM competency:
    - certification
    - standard assessments
    - experience
    - pre-contract BIM Execution Plan
    - example BIM models

- The gold standard for BIM competency would include elements all five methods of assessment. But, it is important that the requested information is bespoke to your needs and addresses your specific BIM requirements. Make sure you don't place unnecessary burdens on your supply chain, do not ask for information if it doesn't directly assist you in assessing BIM competency for your project.

- You need to follow up on BIM competency by including your BIM deliverables within your contract documents. This will require professional legal advice.

CHAPTER 8: CLASSIFICATIONS

Classification - The action or process of classifying something. A category into which something is put. (Oxford Dictionaries)

WHAT IS A CLASSIFICATION SYSTEM?

Classification is a method of putting something into a group or category. Grouping things together is very natural to us. We find it easy, sometimes too easy, to group things. We group people according to nationality, gender or race, we group movies according to genres, ratings or director and we group cars according to engine type, manufacturer and use.

Categorisation happens all the time in the real world. We are always developing new classifications that enable us to group together people. It often happens around election times when we have seen new groups of target voters. In 2013, as the UK Conservative Party identified six key groups of voters; anxious aspirationals, in play centre, steady conservatives, disaffected tories, young inner-city dwellers and urban strugglers. The grouping of voters allows us to develop a mental model of the different groups which helps us to understand the differences and the motivations of each of the groups.

Classifications can be binary, something either fits clearly within one classification or another classification. However, it's usually not that simple. Often, examples will not fit completely within one group, but will have shared traits. We still like to use a single classification, but the one that fits best becomes subjective.

WHY USE CLASSIFICATIONS?

Classifications make it easier for us to manage our data. Non-fiction books in libraries are classified using the Dewey Decimal Classification system, locating relevant books within libraries (and certainly pre-internet) was made significantly easier with the classification system.

Classifications, both formal and informal, are widely used throughout most if not all business sectors. When you become aware of the basics of what a classification system is, you notice them everywhere. Amazon adds the items that it sells to categories. Cars are categorised according to their use, small family, large family, MPV, 4WD, estate and people carrier. Our houses are categorised into bands for the amount of council tax that we pay.

> *Classifications enable us to group together similar items within our BIM models.*

This could be grouping together similar spaces or similar objects.

We add classification tags to the spaces and objects so we can search effectively within the model.

Ideally, the classification tags we add to our spaces and objects are selected from a standard, widely used list of classifications. Although, this isn't always the case. A standard classification system may not be suitable for your needs if, for example, it doesn't contain the groupings you require, so you would need a full or partial bespoke classification system.

Classification systems ensure that the naming, spelling and referencing of similar things is consistent A window inside a building could be described as a glazed screen or an internal window, classification provides those similar objects with a consistent reference and name. Within Uniclass 2015 this would be: *Ss_25_30_95_41* Internal window systems. By using a classification system, we avoid relying on people to use consistent terminology.

It can be confusing to understand why models require any form of classification.

When we look at our models, using the various viewing applications available to us, we nearly always know what every part of the model is. We know that a door is a door and not a section of wall. We know that the beam below a floor is a piece of steelwork for supporting the slab above and that it is an essential part of the design.

But the applications for viewing the model and applications for analysing models do not know this. They can only understand what they have been taught to do. And we are still a long way away from having an application for analysing the visual parts of a model that can automatically assess all the model's internal windows.

Even if we reach that point, the application will still apply a classification to each object, it's just that you may not be aware that this has taken place. Until applications can reliably provide automatic classifications, we need our designers to provide classifications for their own objects.

BENEFITS OF BIM CLASSIFICATION SYSTEM

We know that classification groups similar things together. For our BIM models, classification provides a consistent and uniform language to identify what an object is.

The consistency of a classification system moves beyond the grouping of objects in a single model. It also provides consistency between all of your projects and all of your BIM models.

This means you can directly compare information between projects. So if you want to know the percentage of circulation spaces such as corridors to occupied spaces in your current project and how this compares with previous projects, this becomes an easy task. Or you could instantly establish the number of distribution boards in a project, which can be used to indicate how many you will have in a new similar project.

The use of classification enables us to search, navigate and analyse data within a model in a simplified way.

The volume of data (objects, spaces and attributes) within the average BIM model is increasing exponentially every couple of years. The amount of data within an average model has surpassed what we are able to manage and analyse using simple tools such as schedules and spreadsheets.

If you know that the classification code for a fire doorset is Pr_30_59_24_28 using the Uniclass 2015 language, then it makes it easy to search your model and retrieve all the information about fire doorsets. This could be the number, location, finish, inspection requirements or any other data that your have added (or contained) within each fire doorset object.

OBJECTIVE CHECKING

Classifications also make it easier to check and validate your data, as explored in Chapter 6: Model checking.

The consistent language of a classification means that you and your designers know you're comparing and checking the same things.

If you want to assess the area of occupied spaces, you can tell what is and isn't an occupied space because your designers have classified all the spaces in your model. You are all interpreting information in the same way, which aids communication and simplifies the design development process.

COMMUNICATING BETWEEN CLASSIFICATION SYSTEMS

Later in this chapter, we look at different types of classification systems used within construction. Having a comprehensive classification system within your model, such as Uniclass 2015, allows the easy implementation of other systems. Other systems such as the BRE Green Guide and SFG20 are effectively alternative ways of classifying. Instead of classifying an object by its type, these systems group objects together by maintenance requirements for SFG20 or environmental rating for the BRE Green Guide.

Other systems can be added to your model through the use of mapping. This involves taking your original classifications and linking each original classification to an item in a new system. For example, the Uniclass 2015: *Cavity wall insulation systems Ss_25_13_50_11*, can be linked to the BRE Green Guide item: *Brickwork outer leaf, insulation, aircrete blockwork inner leaf, cement mortar, plaster, paint, element number 806170028*.

Mapping means that it's not necessary to manually add a reference to every single object. It allows a significant proportion of such a task to be automated.

Not everything will map exactly, if everything did, we would just have a universal classification system. But, it will greatly simplify the implementation of other types of systems.

CLASSIFICATION AND MANAGING YOUR FACILITY

You may have plans for a comprehensive and thorough Computer-Aided Facility Management (CAFM) system that will provide you with the tools to effectively manage your estate and this should be an essential part of your strategy. Classifications give you useful information within your CAFM system, plus many other benefits that will massively expand the use of your model data.

It's quite easy to make sure your project model is developed so it meets your current needs, such as integration into your CAFM system. It's quite another challenge to develop a model that will remain useful throughout the life of your asset. And that's the real benefit of applying comprehensive classifications.

Some examples of how classifications can help:

- Assessing areas of volume, such as the total area or all the locations of carpeted finishes within your facility.
- You could apply maintenance best-practice guidelines, such as SFG20.
- Classification future-proofs your data, as it is a relatively simple task to map existing classifications to any future system.
- It provides flexibility so you can implement any new and unforeseen requirements such as statutory requirement and organisational KPIs.
- It enables you to track and manage all your assets, beyond just managing those assets that require maintenance.
- You can ask questions about your facility in complex ways without requiring manual checks. For example, how many doors do you have with closers on to classroom spaces? How many columns are there within 0.5m of a window? What is the clear area outside all platform lift doors?
- When decommissioning your facility and the end of its lifespan, you can assess the volumes of different material types.

COLLABORATION

As looked at above, adding classifications gives you with direct benefits during the design phase and throughout the life of your facility.

However, classifications also benefit the construction delivery team, during the procurement of materials and subcontractors. The consistent grouping of objects mean materials that will always be part of a subcontractor package can easily be extracted, analysed and included within a procurement package. For example, all timber skirting, architrave, window boards and doorsets could be grouped into a joinery subcontractor package. It also helps the overall management of procurement by making it easy to establish which objects within a model have been included in subcontractor packages and which have yet to be procured.

Classifications can do so much more. Mapping the classifications to the RIBA New Rules of Measurement (NRM) codes will simplify measurement and surveying. And grouping objects into classifications helps to programme the works in a similar way to how classification assists with procurement.

CONSTRUCTION CLASSIFICATION SYSTEMS

We have an ISO for construction classification: *ISO 12006-2 Building construction - Organization of information about construction works - Part 2: Framework for classification of information.*

This document, which is available in the UK as *BS ISO 12006-2:2015*, details why we need standardisation within the construction industry, stating:

Building information modelling, in particular, is about exchanges of information of all types along the project timeline and between participants and applications. For this exchange to be successful, a complete and consistent approach to construction object classification is required within the project, and between projects.

There are many classification systems that we use in construction. In the UK, we provide new buildings with an energy rating classification. From G, the worst score, through to A for the most energy-efficient buildings. Timber used in construction has a C classification or a rating depending upon its intended use. There are many many more, for steelwork, risk, colours, slip resistance, BREEAM... the list can go on and on.

However, what we are primarily looking at here is a building-wide classification system focusing on the things that make up a building - the spaces and individual parts of a building.

When it comes to building-wide classification systems, the list is more limited. In the UK the options tend to consist of Uniclass, CAWS (common arrangement of works systems), NRM (New Rules of Measurement), CI/SfB (Construction Index/ Samarbetskommitten for Byggnadsfragor) and Omniclass.

Uniclass, for the reasons provided below, is our preferred classification system at BIMsense. But, it's useful to consider each system and how the system developed.

UNICLASS

Uniclass is a UK-specific classification system. The original version, Uniclass 1, was developed by the Construction Project Information Committee (CPIC) and published in 1997. Uniclass broadly follows the guidance of *BS ISO 12006-2:2015* the British Standard framework for classifying information about construction works.

It's generally considered the most current system available and has improved on other legacy and current systems.

As part of the UK government's BIM Level 2 mandate, Uniclass became embedded within its requirements. This was after the ongoing development of Uniclass was handed over to the NBS.

We are now onto Uniclass 2, which has the official name of Uniclass 2015.

Uniclass currently consists of 11 tables:

Co - Complexes

- En - Entities
- Ac - Activities
- SL - Spaces/ locations
- EF - Elements/ functions
- Ss - Systems
- Pr - Products
- TE - Tools and Equipment
- PM - Project management
- Zz - CAD
- FI - Form of information - please note that at the time of writing, this table remains in beta.

Uniclass 2015 is very much a live system, with regular updates that generally add classifications or amend technical errors, rather than altering existing codes.

New codes are often added following consultation or feedback from other organisations. The October 2017 update to the Ss - Systems table added new codes following requests from Highways England and Transport for London, which makes it clear that there are large UK organisations using, or planning to use, the Uniclass 2015 classification.

Each of the Uniclass 2015 tables consists of a hierarchical arrangement.

The initial two-letter classification code describes the table as listed above, for example, any code starting with Pr would be from the products table.

A TYPICAL UNICLASS 2015 CODE HIERARCHY

Object level: A typical code is *Pr_30_36_08_24* - the code for door latches. This is the most detailed code level and is described as the object level.

Section level: By going one level higher to *Pr_30_36_08*, to the section level, this code describes bolting, latching and locking hardware. It contains door latches, plus other bolting, latching and locking hardware such as barrel bolts *Pr_30_36_08_06,* and digital door locks *Pr_30_36_08_21.*

Sub-group level: The next level up from the section level is the sub-group level, following the above code, we get *Pr_30_36* which is described as hardware products. Within this group, we have the above bolting, latching and locking hardware item, plus general hardware *Pr_30_36_33* and hinges and hanging hardware *Pr_30_36_36,* which both contain their own section codes and the object codes.

Group level: The highest level within each table is the group level. *Pr_30* is the group code for opening products. Other group level codes include *Pr_20* structure and general products, and *Pr_35* services distribution products.

Pr_30	Opening products	Group Level
Pr_30_36	Hardware products	Sub-group Level
Pr30_36_08	Bolting, latching and locking hardware	Section Level
Pr_30_36_08_24	Door latches	Object Level

Some of the tables have a hierarchical structure with parent-child relationships, although using database terminology, the tables would be linked with a many-to-many relationship - when a parent row in the table has a relationship with several child rows in the table, and vice versa. For example the En - Entities table describes types of facilities. The Entities table includes the codes *En_25_10_70* tertiary educational buildings and *En_25_30_40* laboratory buildings.

Tertiary educational buildings contain spaces. The spaces within the buildings can each be classified using codes from the SL - Spaces/locations table. The building could contain enclosed offices *SL_20_15_27*, classrooms *SL_25_10_14* and lecture theatres *SL_25_10_47*.

As an example of a many-to-many relationship outside of construction consider books and authors - each book may have one or more authors, and each author may have written multiple books.

The many-to-many relationship occurs because buildings usually contain many spaces. But, an enclosed office can also occur in many different type of buildings.

The main result of the many-to-many relationships between tables is that if you look at a code within one table you cannot assume that it will align with another table.

For example, the system code *Ss_30* refers to roof, floor and paving systems, but it's not possible to look at another table for 30 codes and assume the relate to each other, the product table *Pr_30* refers to Opening products. This makes the tables more difficult to navigate, but it's unavoidable due to the detail of the classification.

The relationships between tables, although implied, is not explicitly listed. You cannot select from a defined list all the possible spaces that could exist within laboratory buildings. This is probably because such a list would be quite subjective - NBS as the owner of the information would have to include all possible options. Individual organisations could be more flexible in their use of the tables and could develop limited selections from other tables.

The tables can be linked in various ways. The following arrangement provides one method or understanding the implicit links between tables:

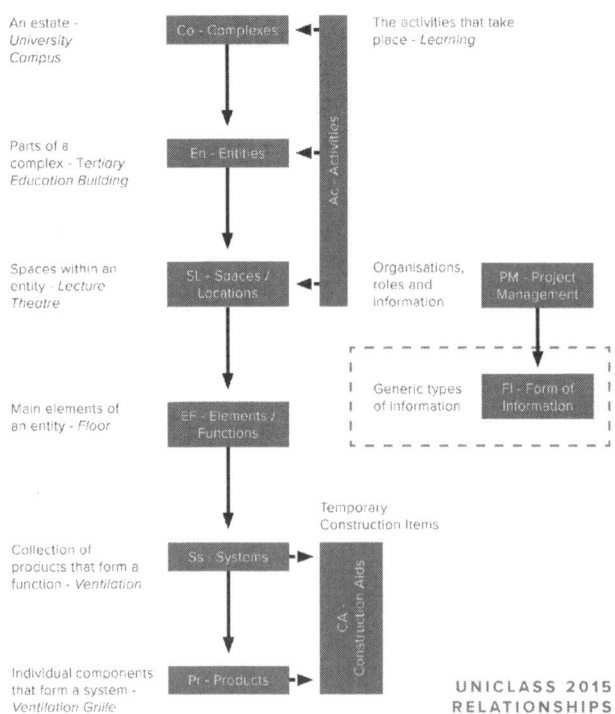

UNICLASS 2015 RELATIONSHIPS

The tables become more detailed as you work down the list from Co - Complexes to Pr - Products (with the exception of the EF - elements/functions table). They start at fewer than 400 individual items and end with almost 7,000 items in the products table.

As with any classification system there are some problems with Uniclass. Some of the descriptions or names of the codes can be ambiguous and it can be difficult to decide where to classify an item. The Pr - Products table has object level codes for both fire doorsets and high security doorsets. It leads to the question, how would you classify a combined high security and fire doorset?

For your organisation, this shouldn't be too much of an issue, as long as you are consistent with the classifications you use. However, the bigger picture of using classifications should enable us to easily compare projects by selecting like-for-like using classifications. Inconsistencies with classifying items will remove some of the anticipated benefits.

NBS, which manages Uniclass 2015, also provides a system of specifying building products. In the years prior to NBS being awarded the responsibility for managing Uniclass 2015, it provided a new specification system, NBS Create, which provided digital integrations and a new referencing system. Previously, NBS used a letter and two-number format (which was aligned to SMM7 - Standard Method of Measurement and CAWS), L10 for Windows / Rooflights / Screens / Louvres and F10 for Brick / Block walling. Each section was followed by various sub-clauses in a three-digit numerical format. NBS Create adopted a a *xx-xx-xx* / xxx format. So *90-40-75 / 320* references flat plate solar collectors. It seems that at some time there was an effort to have logical links between the NBS Create and Uniclass 2015, as some of the numbers for some of the codes are similar. But, my guess is that due to different release dates, they were unable to align the systems, which is a shame as it would have provided significant benefits.

You need to be really clear that NBS Create and Uniclass 2015 (which are both provided by NBS) are not the same thing. Even though the codes may have some similarity, they are different systems and they are used for different purposes.

NBS has attempted to provide some clarity by including the mapping of some of the codes from the Ss - Systems and Pr - Products table to the NBS Create references. The mapping references are provided within the freely available spreadsheet downloads from the NBS mini site, the NBS BIM toolkit. The Ss - Systems table spreadsheet also provides mapping to New Rules of Measurement (NRM), which is detailed separately below.

OMNICLASS

Omniclass is a fully fledged classification system. Omniclass originates from North America and can be viewed as the North American version of Uniclass 2015. It heavily borrowed many of the principles of Uniclass 1, but this also meant that in some cases it inherited some of the problems of Uniclass 1.

In a similar way to Uniclass 2015, Omniclass follows the high-level requirements of *ISO 12006-2*, although the references within the two classifications are completely different. The ISO just provides the detail of how a classification system should be arranged and what it should contain.

There are some earlier tables and classifications systems that are no longer used, but are either included within Omniclass or have been superseded by Omniclass, such as Uniformat and MasterFormat.

Omniclass has 15 tables:

Construction entities by function – Table 11.

Construction entities by form – Table 12.

Spaces by function – Table 13.

Spaces by form – Table 14.

Elements (includes designed elements) – Table 21.

Work results – Table 22.

Products – Table 23.

Phases – Table 31.

Services – Table 32.

Disciplines – Table 33.

Organisational roles – Table 34.

Tools – Table 35.

Information – Table 36.

Materials – Table 41.

Properties – Table 49.

Omniclass is a very mature and comprehensive classification system. It uses a fully numerical classification method, which has some benefit over the mixed alphanumeric Uniclass 2015 system. The highest level code refers in a very rational way to the table.

Like Uniclass 2015, Omniclass uses hierarchical levels. But, whereas Uniclass 2015 is consistent in assigning the most detailed code for each table to the location where an object or activity is placed (with all the higher levels providing parent grouping), Omniclass does not have this consistency. You cannot be sure if you have reached the lowest child level due to the inconsistency of the depth of classification within each table.

Omniclass also has some missing tables, when compared with the Uniclass 2015 tables - it doesn't have any tables that can be directly related with the Uniclass 2015 Co - Complexes, Ac - Activities and Ss - Systems. Unlike the Uniclass 2015 PM - Project management table, which includes organisational roles and information deliverables, Omniclass effectively separates these into three separate tables (Table 33 - Disciplines, Table 34 - Organisational Roles and Table 36 - Information)

The development of Omniclass is also a little uneven. Development appears to be proportionate to the input provided from different sectors within the construction industry. Table 13 - Spaces by function has almost 50% of the possible codes specific to health projects.

it also suffers with the same problem as Uniclass 2015, in that there are countless many-to-many relationships that make full alignment impossible, without introducing duplicates which introduce a whole level of new problems.

Again, like Uniclass 2015, Omniclass is a live system. The last update to Omniclass was in 2013, when Table 11 was updated, and all but three of the tables were updated during 2012. One of the biggest problems with Omniclass updates is that they have altered the coding of existing classifications. This has been avoided within Uniclass 2015 due to the more structured approach of having consistent child levels within each table. Changing codes means that information currently classified with Omniclass coding may become outdated and may require maintenance to keep your data useful.

The final consideration of Omniclass is that it has (quite understandably) a North American bias. This means it is unlikely to include any UK-specific construction references, for example, taps rather than faucets, and that some spellings will not be consistent, for example, labor rather than labour, center rather than centre.

COMMON ARRANGEMENT OF WORK SECTIONS (CAWS)

Common Arrangement of Work Sections (CAWS) was first published in 1987, and its last update was in 1997. The update was provided to align CAWS with the (then new) Uniclass 1.

The aim of CAWS was to provide standardisation, and this was largely achieved with its widespread adoption. NBS, SMM7 (Standard Method of Measurement), Spons and Wessex (price books) all followed the CAWS template. CAWS was and is very much a child of its time. It was groundbreaking and relevant at the time it was produced, providing a unified approach to the description of work sections.

CAWS consists of around 360 work sections and 26 high-level sections. Typical work sections included:

A10 - Project particulars

A44 - Temporary works

C10 - Site survey

E20 - Formwork for in situ concrete

F10 - Brick/block walling

H11 - Curtain walling

K40 - Demountable suspended ceilings

N10 - General fixtures/furnishings/equipment

X10 - Lifts

Z10 - Purpose-made joinery

Over time, the limitations of CAWS have become evident. The single table is made up of a mixture of activities and objects. Its 360 work sections limited flexibility and expansion. And it was never intended to be a full construction classification system, it was an early approach to sort and arrange construction activities and objects.

The CAWS coding system is very familiar, if not the origin of the system. The CAWS references will probably continue to persist, but it really doesn't have any use within BIM. We are looking here at classification systems for use within BIM, which means that all objects (assets, spaces, facilities and systems), activities and types of information are able to be classified or grouped. CAWS doesn't have any classifications for the use of a space or a facility. And where it does provide a reference for a type of object, such as K40 demountable suspended ceilings, it only provides only a very broad classification.

If you are looking to future-proof your organisational information you need to implement a more detailed classification system than the one available through the static and increasingly irrelevant CAWS.

CONSTRUCTION INDEX / SAMARBETSKOMMITTEN FOR BYGGNADSFRAGOR (CI/SFB)

Construction Index / Samarbetskommitten for Byggnadsfragor (CI/SfB) can be considered the great grandfather of construction classification systems. It is the original construction classification that has influenced all the current systems. It was established in 1959 as a Scandinavian classification system.

It's often used within architectural design practices whose members want to classify their libraries of information, especially drawing references. It also went on to directly inform standards such as BS 1192-5:1990 for construction information, which has now been superseded.

It's a complex system, which often resulted in only a partial implementation. However, you may come across this system if you encounter references such as 31.4 for window openings.

It has been adapted and evolved by many organisations. Architectural drawings have traditionally included a series of numbers, to group together similar types of drawings, which were loosely based on CI/SfB:

00 - Existing

01 - GA plans

03 - GA sections

09 - Fire strategy

20 - Detail location

31 - External doors and windows

32 - Internal doors and windows

35 - Ceilings

70 - Room elevations

71 - Signage

90 - External

You have probably come across various versions of the above list. All slightly different with alterations to the numbering or the wording. Its widespread use indicates that it was clearly a useful method to organise information. However, the limitations of the system lead to adaptations by individual organisations. And as soon as a system becomes non-standard and bespoke, the wider benefits are lost.

The system hasn't been updated for decades. It should not be considered for a robust classification system, or for one you want to be future-proof..

NEW RULES OF MEASUREMENT (NRM)

New Rules of Measurement (NRM) is a three-volume set of measurement rules, designed to provide comprehensive measurement rules and cost management guidance.

The intention of NRM is that it remains independent of the classification system, but has the ability to be mapped to whatever classification is used by a project.

Volume 1 provides a full schedule of codes that groups building elements in a way that simplifies quantifying and costing a facility. The coding has a familiar look with three levels (group, element and sub-element):

1.1.1 Standard foundations

2.1.4 Concrete frames

2.7.1 Walls and partitions

2.6.2 External doors

2.8.1 Internal doors

3.1.1 Wall finishes

8.3.2 External planting

The elemental breakdown is specifically designed for elemental cost planning and not as a full classification system. For example, when mapping 1.1.1 Standard foundations to the Uniclass 2015 Ss - Systems table we get 11 different codes, such as *Ss_20_05_15_70* Reinforced concrete pad and strip foundation systems and *Ss_20_05_50_65* Precast concrete foundation and plinth systems.

One interpretation of this is that the simpler NRM codings will be sufficient for your needs. But that misses the main point of what the two systems are attempting to achieve. If we return to our original definition of a classification system, it attempts to group together similar things. NRM does this, so it does provide a form of classification. However, its purpose is to group things together to enable measurement and elemental costings to be easier and more structured.

NRM does not attempt to provide groupings for other purposes. It doesn't provide a specific coding for a type of standard foundation or indeed the components contained within a foundation, because it doesn't need to. It also does not code things that aren't relevant for measurement and costing purposes, such as the function of a building, the function of a space or the type of organisation.

I'm sure a significant number of organisations will use NRM codings as their preferred system of classification. Using NRM isn't a bad thing, it will produce codings for most, if not of all, of a buildings systems. But, it won't enable classification of a whole project, which will undoubtedly lead to restrictions in the future.

OTHER CLASSIFICATION SYSTEMS

There are many other classification systems that could be used within the construction industry which I have not looked at in detail, such as BSAB (a Swedish system), DBK (a Danish system), STLB (a German system) and STABU (a Dutch system).

You may come across project information that uses more than one classification system. You may request the use of Uniclass 2015 codes, while your project quantity surveyor may require CAWS. This shouldn't be a problem for your project model. It's acceptable within Industry Foundation Classes (IFC) to have more than one classification for individual objects. For clarity within the completed asset model, you could request that other classifications are removed from your model prior to handover.

BESPOKE CLASSIFICATION SYSTEM

The final option available to you when considering a classification system is to use your own bespoke system, although, it's not one that I would recommend unless you have a specific reason.

Let's understand why you would want to use your own classification system. You may already have a system in place, it may be embedded into your processes and may have worked successfully over many years.

If your needs are limited (and probably very limited), there may be not be sufficient reasons for you to change your current system.

However, just because something has worked successfully in the past, doesn't mean it will continue to be suitable for your future needs. If you don't believe you'll need to manage your assets in a more intelligent way in the future, or that you'll have no reason to automate and digitise your future processes, then continue as you are.

Whatever you decide to do, please don't consider setting up a bespoke system if you don't currently have your own working system in place.

Your own system will require a wide consultation to ensure it works for everyone in your organisation. It will need someone to own the system, to develop it and most importantly to maintain and update it.

Everything requires maintenance, including a bespoke classification system, otherwise over time it will start falling apart, it will stop working, it will devalue and eventually it will stop being used and will no longer provide any value or benefit.

This applies to everything - your facilities, the assets within your facilities and your data (and also to yourself!).

It also explains why some of the legacy classification systems, Uniclass 1, CAWS, CI/SfB, have become increasingly irrelevant over time, in contrast to Uniclass 2015 and Omniclass, which are current and remain relevant because they have recently been updated or maintained.

If you do already have a working bespoke system in place, you could consider an orderly transfer to a new classification system. Your project models could initially contain your own classifications as well as a standard classification system. Models can contain multiple classification systems, and it's entirely possible and achievable to have more than one classification applied to the assets within your models. This will enable your existing systems to continue working while you lay the foundations for using a new system.

CLASSIFICATIONS WITHIN YOUR MODEL

In this section I will use Uniclass 2015 for the examples and methods for classifications within your model. In some cases, the examples can be directly applied to other classification systems, definitely Omniclass, but older classifications systems will not be suitable for all of the examples and methods below.

PRODUCT AND SYSTEM CODES

Objects within your model can be classified in a number of ways. You can classify an object according to its component parts (or using Uniclass speak, its products). Or you can use a classification that applies to a wider grouping or products, that links objects by the system they are within.

Doors or component door parts within your facility should be classified according to their specific type. This could be *Pr_30_59_23_96 Wood door frames*, *Pr_30_59_23_53 Metal door leaves* or *Pr_30_59_24_28 Fire doorsets*.

It's also possible to apply more than one product classification to a single object, depending upon the detail within the object, although, using the correct IFC method of applying classifications this does require a technical workaround which is beyond the scope of this book.

Your doorset may be a single object that includes the frame, door leaf and ironmongery. At least three product codes could be applied to the single door object, although you could apply more as the ironmongery can split further into hinges, door closer and lever handle. You may not be able to see all these items when viewing your model, but that doesn't really matter. You can use your data, your classifications, to establish what products can be found within your facility.

It would be also useful if there was an easy way to group all your doors together. You may think that the higher-level common product code grouping, in this example *Pr_30_59*, would provide the grouping for all your doors. But, *Pr_30_59* describes openings and opening component products, which also contains many non-door related products such as *Pr_30_59_01_96 wheelchair ramps* and *Pr_30_59_07_72 roller blinds*. So a search for all products within and below the coding *Pr_30_59* would provide doors and many other items that are not doors.

This is why it's useful to apply system codes to all your objects. For standard doors and door components you would also add the code *Ss_25_30_20_25 doorset systems*. Non-standard doors such as roller shutters would have a different system coding *Ss_25_30_20_74 roller shutter doorset systems*. And all types of doors are available within the *Ss_25_30_20 door, shutter and hatch systems code*.

The system's coding will make it easy to assess other groupings such as all the external walls, all the external windows or all the internal doors.

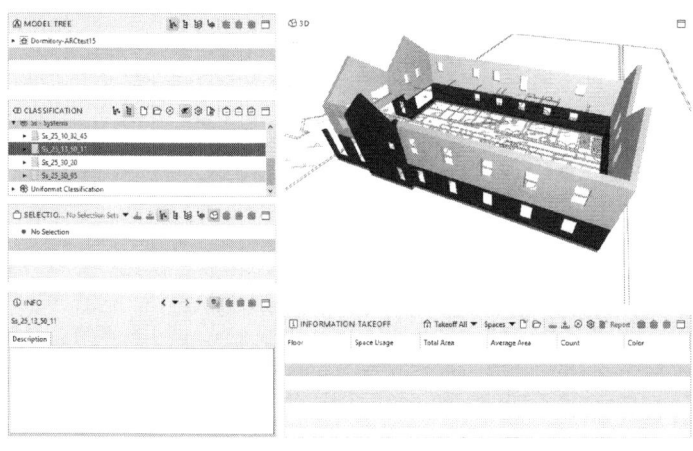
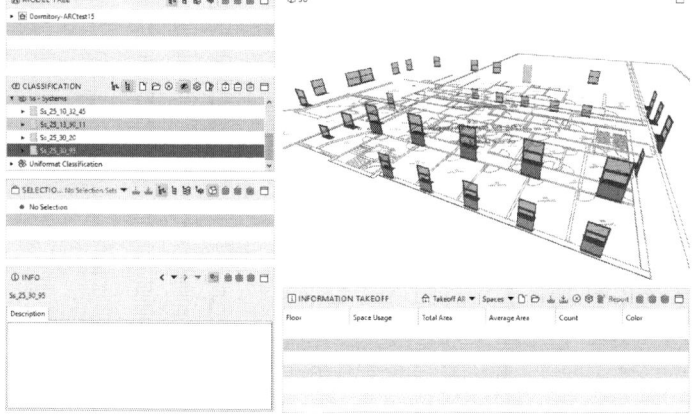
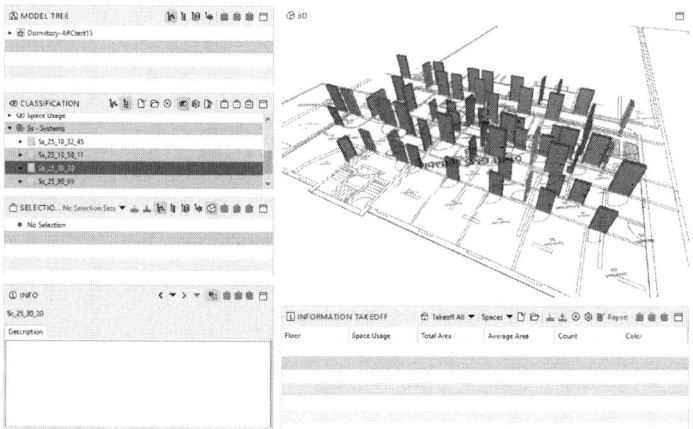

FACILITY AND SPACE CODES

It's also beneficial to add codes that group together your type of facility or the type of space within your facility. Uniclass 2015 provides the En - Entities table for your facility type and SL - Spaces/locations for the space types.

Your estate could require a more complex level of classification than the available codings can provide. If this is the case, it is useful to add more than one set of classifications. You can do this by providing a standard classification, such as Uniclass 2015, that can be easily understood by all stakeholders and an organisational-specific code for your specific use.

The most flexible and suitable way of adding classifications to your model is to use the predefined IFC structure, specifically the IfcClassification and IfcClassificationReference entities. IfcClassification provides the detail of the classification system, Uniclass 2015 or Omniclass and the version numbers. IfcClassificationReference provides the specific reference code and description such as *Ss_25_30_20_25 Doorset systems*.

APPLYING CLASSIFICATIONS

It can be difficult in some circumstances to assess the correct classification code that should be applied. Some objects may fall within two different classification codes and some classification descriptions are open to interpretation. What if I have a door that is both a *Ss_25_30_20_38 high speed doorset systems* and also an *Ss_25_30_20_45 loading bay doorset systems*? This is an example where both codes should be applied to the object, it's the belt and braces approach.

Ambiguous classification descriptions are not quite as easy to resolve. If you encounter a description that is not clear, then as an organisation you should record whatever decision you make. It won't matter too much what the decision is, so long as you can consistently apply the decision in the future.

CHAPTER SUMMARY

We add classification tags to spaces and objects to enable us to effectively search within the model. Classification systems ensure that the naming and referencing of similar things is consistent, it ensures that we don't use different names or spellings to similar objects

- I recommend the consistent use of Uniclass 2015 for classifying your model. Objects within your model can be classified with both Product (Pr) and System (Ss) classifications

- Consistent and thorough use of Uniclass 2015 will allow the implementation of other systems through mapping. More than one classification system can be applied to your model, provided you take a consistent approach.

Classifications will provide benefits through all project stages, design, construction and operation, for you and all your stakeholders, designers, contractors and suppliers.

CHAPTER 9: RISK

Risk - *A situation involving exposure to danger. The possibility of financial loss.* (Oxford Dictionaries)

RISK AND YOUR MODEL

Your model can become an effective tool for managing project risks during the design and construction process and later managing risks associated with running your facility.

All large organisations are risk averse. When you're working for a large organisation - especially when you're making significant investment decisions such as developing a new facility - you will be required to assess all significant risks and reduce or eliminate them where possible.

Organisations do not want surprises. They expect all probable project risks to have been identified and assessed. For large and complicated projects this can be an extremely complex task, as risks will be generated from multitudes of places, from design decisions to financing options, cash flow, demand forecasting, legislation, and micro and macro economic impacts, among many others.

> *The general strategy behind managing risks within your project model is to reduce the amount of uncontrolled and chaotic information.*

It's about applying order to our current fragmented and subjective processes.

We have to get better at identifying, analysing and mitigating for project risks. Extensive research from 2015 by Glenigan, using data from Constructing Excellence, the Construction Industry Training Board and the Department for Business, Innovation and Skills, found that only 40% of projects were completed on time. This means it's more likely than not that your current project will overrun. The same research also found 31% of projects go over budget.

The effects of cost and time overruns are enormous. It's all too easy to think that they only happen to other projects. There is a very real chance that they will happen on your project. For you as an individual it won't be easy to do things in a different way, but you have to ask yourself how important it is to you that your project is a success.

Not all risks are suitable for managing within your model, but for those that are, your model can provide an integrated approach. It allows all stakeholders to understand and comment on the project risks, it simplifies the process and it in the near future it will lead to automatically identifying risks by analysing project models.

RESIDUAL RISKS

Chapter 2: BIM: The container for your data looked at the management of residual risks through your model. Residual risks are those risks that will remain with a facility during its operational life. These are the risks that have not been, or could not be, eliminated during the design development process.

In Chapter 2, I discussed the ways residual risks can be associated with objects, spaces or the facility as a whole. By locating risks within the model, we can understand the relationships between risks, objects and locations. It provides an effective way of assessing risks because it lets us view the risks as they are related to our digital model, and identify unacceptable residual risks, as well as those risks that will become an unnecessary burden on the users of the building and its maintenance staff.

It also provides a unified way of collating residual risks. You will often find that different designers will employ different techniques for recording residual risks. Some will provide a schedule of risks, while others will add residual risks to 2D plans. Both of these techniques generate isolated "dumb data". The information itself will be valid and useful, but in these formats the data is dumb in the sense that it doesn't link or directly relate to other data.

The current process of assessing risk with isolated dumb data also adds to all the other isolated dumb data. At the end of each project stage, enormous amounts of isolated report information is produced by the professional team. The volume of information makes it difficult to assess objectively and also difficult to focus on the important parts.

By integrating risk information within your model, you reduce the amount of isolated data; you transfer the information into the model, which enables you to perform sophisticated, intelligent searches and interrogations.

By locating your risk data within your model it becomes intelligent. It has defined relationships with the model. This makes it easier to assess whether risks remain relevant and whether the developing design will have an effect on a risk.

For example, a facility's atrium space could have a residual risk for high-level access. This risk will be available to view within a shared model. By making the risk available for other designers to view, design decisions can be made that will reduce hazards. Building services that require regular planned maintenance could be located at a lower level. This will lower the overall effect of the risk, as access should be very limited.

You can manage risk within your model by using the IFC risk property set. An IFC risk could be a generic risk that is applied to multiple objects and spaces, or it could be very specific and only occur in a unique scenario.

The IFC risk approach will enable you to assess your model in various ways. You could view all the locations where an individual type of risk occurs, and this could be done by highlighting the relevant spaces or objects. You could view all the risks together. You will also be able to export the risks into a more traditional schedule, enabling further analysis.

COLLABORATION

> *The risk information within your shared models will be available to your whole project team and all project stakeholders.*

This will lead to a fully informed team, provide a catalyst for discussion and help the team to make the best decisions for mitigating risks. Sharing risks within your model also ensures that risks remain relevant - if an object or space with risks is removed, the associated risks are removed. You can also analyse changes to your project model and assess their effect on associated risks.

> *The sharing of information and your project model as a single source of truth remain the main benefits of BIM.*

We are attempting to remove the existing silos that exist within the disjointed construction process. Organisations often focus on their own specific issues and risks, which are only occasionally relevant to the project. This is a completely understandable approach - as individuals, we tend to be employed primarily by organisations rather than by projects. So if there is a conflict between an action that benefits our organisation or one that benefits a project, we tend to prioritise our employer.

Managing project risks within the model means that risks are wholly focused on the project. Collaboratively sharing the risks within the model widens accountability and provides an impetus for developing collaborative solutions, sometimes novel, but always project focused.

It's also beneficial to coordinate and manage project risks within a model from the earliest stages of a project through to completion. There are two main advantages to following this consistent approach:

1. As a project progresses through its stages, its number of risks tends to increase substantially. This isn't due to an increase in the overall risk of a project, but is due to the increasing project detail providing more clarity of where risks occur. Ideally, we don't want to filter out risks by subjectively omitting risks from a project model. We should aim to include all applicable risks and apply filters when assessing and viewing risks.

2. It enables us to track risks and understand the associated decisions. This provides a useful audit trail, as well as valuable data that can be applied to other projects.

RISK CALIBRATION

As humans we are very poor at assessing risks. We find it really difficult to put risk in context and apply accurate measurements.

In the United States, figures from the National Safety Council show that we are approximately 100 times more likely to die while travelling in a car than when travelling in an airplane. Yet, perhaps because we rarely hear about the regular traffic accidents that consistently result in fatalities, the risk of travelling by car doesn't normally enter our consciousness. In contrast, news sources tend to give significant coverage to stories of a single aircraft accident that results in multiple fatalities. This information becomes our source for calibrating the risks of travel: we hear about aircraft accidents; we don't often hear about traffic accidents, therefore aircraft travel is riskier. This type of information provides us with incorrect mental shortcuts.

An example from the book *Homo Deus: A Brief History of Tomorrow*, by Yuval Noah Harari, is that in 2012, about 56 million people died throughout the world: 620,000 died from human violence (war killed 120,000, crime 500,000). Whereas 800,000 committed suicide and 1.5 million died from diabetes. And if you look at global figures from 2010, obesity and related illnesses killed about 3 million people, terrorists killed 7,697. So you are almost 400 times more likely to die from overeating than you are from a terrorist attack, yet how many of us think about the risk of eating a tasty dessert after our meal, compared with our preoccupation with the threat of terrorism?

This leads into how we assess project risks.

We are likely to take the same approach that we do in our everyday life when we assess the risks associated with our projects. We are more likely to apply a higher weighting to risks that we have encountered previously, or ones that we are familiar with, than to other less obvious risks.

In Douglas W Hubbard's book *How to Measure Anything*, the author recommends a calibration exercise to enable us to better assess risks. This involves considering the extreme outcomes of an uncertain event, such as the financial loss of not being able to use a facility if an air-handling unit fails, then gradually closing in on a more realistic figure. Clearly, an even better approach would be take the assessment of the risk away from us humans and instead let actual data provide the assessment of the risk.

Douglas W Hubbard also recommends that we should be clear in our definition of risk, so we can provide an accurate method of measurement, if risk is a state of uncertainty that could result in an undesirable outcome such as financial loss or injury, the measurement of risk applies a possibility against the undesirable outcome.

It's important for us to be able to assess risks as accurately as we can and use objective methods for measuring risk where possible.

OBJECTIVE RISK ASSESSMENT

Your model can be the basis for objectively assessing risk. At present we tend to focus on the risks that we are aware of, usually ones we have experienced first hand. But, throughout our working life, we probably only see a handful of projects right through from the start of design to handover, which means our awareness of possible risks is limited.

We should use different and objective methods to ensure that all possible risks are assessed equally and without bias.

If risks are managed and integrated within our model, we can apply objective measurements to those risks. As a simple example, it would mean the assessment of an atrium that requires high-level access to maintain building services equipment could be based on actual data, such as the number of incidents that occur when accessing building services at high level.

We may find that maintenance access for a certain type of building service has a far higher risk than other types of building services. This will result in design decisions that focus on eliminating hazards that have the highest risk.

This type of data is not yet widely available and it has to become a long-term goal for the whole of the industry. Once the wider industry adopts multiple digital models containing this type of information and accurately records incidents, we will reach a critical mass of data that will result in informed and accurate risk reduction.

MODEL ANALYSIS RISK ASSESSMENT

Assessment of risks should not stop at the risks we can identify. Instead, we should assess risks by analysing our digital models. We want our analysis of risk to inform us of where our project will fail before it fails. We want to be informed where programmes will overrun and where design will stall, so we can make plans to avoid the avoidable.

The assessments should fully objective without bias,to allow us to focus on the critical risks. The risk analysis should also take into account the design progress, and identify whether an area of design has fallen behind programme. This is especially important when specific delays in making design decisions could have an effect on the completion of a project. It's all too easy to think that delays during the design stages are less important than delays during the construction process, even though they could both affect the completion date and delays during design often decrease the time available for later stages.

We should be analysing our models using algorithms. Algorithms are a series of logical instructions that can be followed by a computer. Algorithms perform the task of analysing our models in a far better way then we can. A computer checks everything that you want to be checked, it won't get bored, distracted or take shortcuts. This enables us to manage projects using an analytical approach and to monitor trends; analytical project management rather than the all-too-common reactive and subjective project management.

We shouldn't need to manually add a risk for accessing building services within an atrium. This should be automatically added to the model, as there is known and recorded risk.

THE FUTURE

I'm confident that we will have automatic model checks that focus on project risks, in the near future. The checks will have the ability to instantly identify a wide range of project risks beyond the health and safety risks, such as:

- **Building location risks:** Environmental factors; local authority planning; traffic predictions; external noise; external factors that may have an effect on the design, construction and operation of a new facility.

- **Health and wellbeing risks:** Occupied rooms without a view out; air pollution pathways; potential for natural ventilation; materials likely to contain Volatile Organic Compounds.

- **Financial risks:** Assessing building materials against current and forecast raw material prices; identifying tasks requiring significant labour resources.

- **Whole-life cost risks:** High maintenance plant and equipment; accurately assessing the optimal time for replacing assets.

- **Building risks:** Building design; compliance with statutory requirements and building regulations; space types with areas above and beyond normal ranges; sufficient amenities for the designed occupancy. Approximately 38% of disputes arise from design related issues - Bramble, BB and Cipollini, M.D. (1995), Resolution of disputes to avoid construction claims.

- **Procurement risks:** Shortages of materials (or even of opportunities due to oversupply); financial risk of supply chain organisations.

- **Operational risks:** Inaccessible or difficult-to-maintain assets.

- **Construction risks:** Safe working areas; risk of trips, slips and falls; lifting constraints; crane manoeuvrability.

To enable unbiased and objective assessments, information will be drawn from external data sources.

HOW TO FUTURE-PROOF YOUR CURRENT MODEL

We don't currently have the tools for automating model risk analysis. Therefore, we should all ensure our project models are being developed in a way, through your EIR guidance, that enables you to use such services when they become available.

> *The three things that will future-proof your model for advanced risk analysis are: the widespread use of a standard classification system; structured data; and a quality graphical model.*

I believe the use of classifications is so important that I have give it its own chapter, as does model quality checking. And structured data is referenced throughout this book. Structured data requires your data to have consistent naming for all objects, spaces and data types, and between designers and projects. It also requires your data attributes to be consistent. The consistency of your attributes, the storage containers for individual pieces of data such as the fire rating of a door, is important to make it easy for applications to locate and make sense of your data. You can ensure consistency of your attributes by using the defined IFC attributes.

MODEL DATA RISK

In this chapter I have focused on how you can use your model for assessing, understanding and managing risks. However, you also need to remember that information within your model may be the cause of risks.

In Chapter 4: Establishing your organisational data requirements, there is an employer purpose section for the management of security and surveillance. This required you to consider information in your model that could be sensitive, and whether this information should not be included within your model.

BIM collaboration could make data too easy to access. This could be sensitive information that could be obtained from high-risk facilities, prisons, police stations, data centres or individual elements of data such as surveillance cameras.

If you have such information within your model you need to ensure that the data is safe and the risks of a security breach are correctly assessed.

This information should be included within your EIR, in the section schedule of any security and integrity requirements for the project which is discussed in the Chapter 11: Employer's Information Requirements (EIR).

CHAPTER SUMMARY

Your model can provide an integrated approach to managing risks. It allows all stakeholders to understand and comment on the project risks, it simplifies the process and in the near future it will lead to automatically identifying risks by analysing project models.

- Risks can be managed using project models by adding risks directly to the spaces or objects to which they apply.

- Models are ideally suited for managing residual risks. You can monitor and assess the risks during design and the risks become available to the users of the facility.

- Models can be assessed using rule-based checks to identify risks. Rule-based checks provide an objective assessment of risk.

- All organisations want to reduce risks, particularly safety and financial risks. Using your model should be one of the tools that you use for managing risks.

CHAPTER 10: DATA MAINTENANCE

Maintenance - The process of preserving a condition or situation or the state of being preserved. The process of keeping something in good condition. (Oxford Dictionaries)

Everything requires maintenance and this includes your data.

Your data model of your new or existing estate should be considered as an asset. Yes, it is a model of your facility and it is only useful because it provides a model representation of the facility. But this doesn't prevent the model from being of value and anything of value should be considered an asset. You have tangible and intangible assets: the tangible assets are physical assets such as your completed facility; and the intangible assets are non-physical assets, such as intellectual property, patents and copyrights, and your data model of the estate.

Why should you treat your model as an asset? To understand why this is an important approach let's look at a physical asset. If you have a new estate, just finished with everything working, fully commissioned and balanced, your facility is at its maximum value. Nothing has broken, nothing requires maintenance, cleaning or replacement. Over time as the facility is used, surfaces will become worn, doors will become damaged, valves will require opening and closing or they will become stuck. It's just the natural way that as time progresses, stuff will stop working, or will become worn out due to constant use. As more time passes and as your facility continues to be used, it will devalue.

> *The only way to reduce this decline in value is to expend money to maintain your asset.*

Exactly the same process applies to your data model. The data within the model, the information about the installed assets and the design of your facility, will be correct and validated at the time that of handover or delivery of the model. This is when your model should provide a fully accurate representation of the physical (graphical) parts of your facility and the information about the parts and use of the facility. This data will also start to devalue over time.

As the parts of your facility are altered, maintained and replaced, the model representation will start to differ from the actual facility. The more the information model differs from your facility, the more the model will devalue.

The only way to prevent your data model from devaluing is to invest in maintaining the data, in exactly the same way as your physical facility requires continual investment. The data should be regularly checked for consistency and accuracy.

There is a definite cost to maintaining data to make sure it remains current and relevant. This is why you should only collect the information you require and nothing more. The more data you have within a model, the greater the task of maintaining that data. It's particularly wasteful to maintain data that you haven't used. You may have collected data for the anticipated life of an asset. But unless you use this data for a particular purpose, such as forecasting future costs for maintaining your physical asset, not only will this be a waste of someone's time it will also cost your organisation. As you swap or change assets, you will be required to also add new anticipated life data to correctly maintain your data. And unless you are using this data effectively, this would be a wasted activity.

Of course, you could decide not to maintain your data, not that I would recommend such an approach. However, if you do take this decision, you should also consider why you need a model of your facility. Obtaining an accurate, data-rich model will add to the cost of your project. It will take time for you and your professional team to establish the detail of the project deliverables. An accurate graphical model should, if your designers are designing in a 3D application, be a natural outcome of the project. But developing the model in a way that will work for other uses beyond just design will add costs to your project. It will require your design team to do things in a slightly different way. If you require fire ratings for internal walls, then you will need to be sure that your walls are separated into the correct unit lengths so when a wall changes from fire rated to non-fire rated, this can be identified with data within your model. Your model will also increase the project costs during the construction phase. This is when the vast majority of your data is added to the model. If you have no intention or no plan in place for managing your data model, which will definitely add to your project costs, then seriously consider removing it as a project deliverable.

It could be that you need a project model to help you to understand what BIM is all about, what it really means. This is a completely acceptable approach to take and provides a good learning opportunity for you and your organisation. If this is the approach you decide to take, then at least for your first project, keep the deliverable simple and clear. This will mean that you will have an accurate model you can learn from, but will not require you to burden your project with additional and unnecessary costs.

RESPONSIBILITY FOR MANAGING YOUR DATA MODEL

Someone needs to have responsibility for your data. Ideally, this will be your organisational information manager. If you don't have an information manager in your organisation, you don't necessarily need to create a new role or a new position, but someone needs to be responsible for your facility's models and information.

Your organisational information manager is the single point of responsibility for your data after it has been delivered, as well as for validating your model and the data at the time of handover. Don't just accept the project model and assume that it will be correct.

Ideally, you will validate your project model at each of the design stages as it would be a really big task to do this all at the completion of your project. To effectively validate your model at each design stage, you need clear project deliverables that identify what will be required at each stage. The correct place for this information, where you will schedule your requirements, will be within your Employer's Information Requirements (EIR).

As your organisational information manager will be the person who validates your project model, they should be fully involved in, or possibly responsible for, developing sections of your EIR. Clear deliverables are essential for an unambiguous and objective validation of data.

Don't forget that your project will also have an appointed project information manager. This should not be the same person as your organisational information manager. All BIM projects, and definitely projects with the Construction Industry Council (CIC) BIM Protocol, will require an information manager for all project stages. A project information manager will be from your professional team. During the early stages, your project information manager could be your lead designer or from a separate specialist BIM consultancy; then during the construction phase your project information manager could be from your main contractor.

The handover validation of your model (which would also normally align closely with the completion of a new facility) should give you a line in the sand when you have confidence that your data is complete and correct. At this time the data should not require any maintenance.

If your information is not accurate at this stage, it's unlikely it ever will be, because as soon as you start using your facility you need to start updating your model to represent the inevitable changes that will take place.

Also don't forget that you will have paid for your data model. You wouldn't accept delivery of any significant physical asset without first checking the item. When you collect your brand new car from the showroom, you look around the car for any damage, you check that everything is in place, such as the spare wheel and you check that the paperwork is correct for tax and ownership. These things come naturally to us for physical assets, but thorough checking is just as essential for non-physical data model assets. You need to check you are being given exactly what you have paid for.

And once again we return to the requirement of clear deliverables (within your EIR), as this is the only way that you will be able to objectively check the model. An ambiguous and vague EIR can only result in ambiguous and vague deliverables. There is chance (a slim chance) that you may be provided with exactly the right information, but why would you leave something as important as your data deliverable to chance, when all it requires are clear deliverables?

Establishing unambiguous deliverables is the only way you will have the authority to ask for any incorrect information to be put right. You will not be able to request, with any authority, that someone corrects your data if you didn't clearly and explicitly identify what you originally wanted. Or, more precisely, without being billed for the cost of correcting the data.

> Don't expect a BMW, but then be disappointed with a Suzuki, if all you asked for was a car.

Everything needs to be clearly specified from the data format, to the attributes that you want for each asset, who provides each item of data and when it's required. This is a very different approach from design-and-build, where we typically leave out specific requirements to enable contractors with their large supply chains to select the most suitable and cost-effective solutions. With BIM, the only cost-effective approach is to detail exactly what you want, this ensures that unnecessary information is not collected and the information is correct at the first attempt.

VALIDATING YOUR DATA MODEL

Validating your data should be a technical and objective exercise. It will involve analysing the data for omissions and errors.

Just to be clear, data validation does not check the quality of the graphical components within your model. Data validation does not check that the graphical model accurately represents the physical model. The graphical model is equivalent to receiving as-built drawings at the completion of a project, the as-built information should be validated by your contractor and your design team. But, it is very sensible to invest some time in checking the graphical accuracy of the model, as you do the data within your model. This can be done by having a requirement within your EIR that the graphical model should be validated by a laser scan of the new facility that produces a point cloud survey. I'm not convinced that the cost of a point cloud survey of a completed asset, for most circumstances, currently justifies the benefits. Alternatively, a sample of measurements should be sufficient for you to have confidence in the quality of the as-built model.

> *The most efficient way of validating your data is to directly compare your requirements with the model data.*

Making direct comparisons of requirements against your model once again comes back to having a clear, detailed and comprehensive information requirements in your EIR.

It's a relatively simple task to extract the data from your model using tools such as Solibri Model Checker or Simplebim, which were examined in Chapter 3: A data-centric culture.

Both allow you to filter and select the actual data that is important for you to check. This will usually be the property sets and the attributes for each of the objects for which you require data. You will have decided, as an organisation, the objects you require data for by working through your employer purposes. This then enables you to select the specific data required for each type of object and for these requirements to be included within your EIR.

The level to which you automate your checks will depend upon the tools available to you and your technical proficiency.

The simplest way is the manual visual check. Let's use a door as an example. By using either of the tools (Solibri Model Checker or Simplebim), you are able to select all the IfcDoor objects within your model and schedule out all the data, all the property sets and attributes for each door. This produces a schedule, in a spreadsheet format, that lists each occurance of a door within your model and all of the attributes for each door.

When it comes to checking the data, you need to check the following:

1. That the objects that require data are represented within the model.
2. That the objects are correctly named.
3. The data attributes required for each type of object are assigned to each object.
4. The data for each attribute has been correctly populated for each object occurrence.

For ease and to avoid confusion and duplicate effort, I suggest that you do not move on to the next type of data check until your current check is 100% correct.

Here's a step-by-step guide:

1. Be sure that all the objects are correctly represented within your model before you start to check that the objects are correctly named.
2. Validate these updates once you have received the updated model with all the correctly assigned objects.
3. Check all newly assigned objects and existing objects for the correct naming.

Checking that objects requiring data are represented within your model is closely associated with the graphical quality of the model. If you can visually see something within the model, then it does exist. But, it's not that unusual for objects to be assigned, during the design stage, with an incorrect IFC entity type. For instance a door within a section of curtain walling could be assigned as *IfcCurtainWall* entity rather than the required *IfcDoor* entity. This wouldn't have any effect when viewing the graphical model, but, it would mean that the underlying data was incorrect.

Your naming requirements - the methodology detailing how objects should be named - depend on your organisational requirements, specifically your existing or proposed CAFM or other data-management systems.

It's a good idea to have a relatively generic naming system that isn't too complicated, but that uniquely names every object requiring data. Each object within your model could consist of a generic group name, such as Door and then a unique number which could assist in locating the object. *Door101* could represent the first occurence of a door on the first floor or your facility and *CurtainWall002* could represent the second curtain wall occurrence on the ground floor of your facility. The name does not need to include other codes that could provide information such as fire rating, because this information will all be contained within specific data attributes.

When we come to the attributes for objects, in the first instance, we are not yet considering whether the specific data is correct. We are not yet checking that the correct fire rating has been provided, we are just checking that an object has a fire rating attribute. An attribute can be considered as the container that will enable a fire rating to be added to a door. The attributes should also be checked for naming errors. Hopefully, your attribute names will follow the IFC framework, although it's possible that you may require unique attributes that aren't available within the standard IFC property sets and attributes. Unique organisational attributes, such as acoustic and fire information for an air transfer grille, will not be standard and this increases the likelihood of naming errors.

For example, from your comprehensive EIR, you will have listed out all the attributes that are required for doors within your model. So, we need to check that each type of attribute has been provided for each door. If you required the fire rating of each door, doors within your model should have the *Pset_DoorCommon* property set and the associated *FireRating* attribute.

Finally, we move on to checking that data has been provided for each of the required object entities. Initially, the check should confirm that data has been provided. This is a compliance check: Has data been provided? The response is yes or no.

Checking that the correct data has been provided is difficult if requiring 100% validation.

Rather than manually checking that every item of data is correct for every object, it should be sufficient to check a sample of data, similar to the approach for checking the graphical accuracy of the model. Depending upon the data type of each attribute, it can also be relatively easy to provide other generic checks. For example, IFC has a standard property set attribute for IfcDoors and IfcWalls that identify if an object is external or internal. The attribute name is IsExternal and the data within this attribute should only consist of a true or false binary response, which is known as a Boolean data type. Any data other than true or false can be rejected. Within Excel, this task can be automated with the conditional formatting function by highlighting all the cells that do not have a Boolean response.

ONGOING MAINTENANCE

Your ongoing data maintenance will be all about putting the right systems in place. This should lead on to supporting behaviours, which ideally results in a culture where maintaining data becomes a normal habit.

Effective data maintenance will require a couple of strategic organisational decisions. These mainly relate to how you will manage significant updates to your estate.

Small changes such as the change of a light fitting (a luminaire) within a suspended ceiling grid from one manufacturer to another should not require any changes to the graphical model. As long as you know you have the light fitting detailed in the correct location, slight alterations to the physical changes aren't, in my opinion, significant enough to require you to alter your graphical model. You would still need to update the data associated with this object however, such as manufacturer, serial number and performance information, but this is significantly easier than updating your graphical model. It's even possible to make these data changes, using tools to amend and update the IFC text file. You can read about the tools that we have developed at BIMsense to for working with IFC files.

Data-only changes mean your team needs to either be able to make the alterations themselves or have an efficient method of reporting back the changes. The best approach is to empower all your team to make small data changes. You can set up a system where changes are limited to certain data fields and any changes are traceable back to the user.

Significant updates include any changes to graphical as well as associated data. These could range from the relocation of a door opening, or the remodelling of a floor, through to an extension to an existing facility.

It's useful to draw a line between your estate's existing buildings that do not have digital data and those that do.

Buildings that have a digital model are likely to be your newer facilities, and they will require all significant changes to be modelled correctly, with the data updated. The responsibility for the graphical updates will need to be established and recorded. This could be an architect for large changes and your modelling technician for smaller changes. You will need to consider whether such changes are undertaken by your own maintenance team or contractors from your supply chain. Where amendments are done by external contractors or consultants, you need to ask how access is provided to your existing data, and how the updated information is received and integrated into your existing applications. Don't forget that the new information will also need to be validated.

For existing facilities that do not currently have digital models, you have two main options. You can continue without digital data, which could be a sensible approach if your maintenance of existing facilities is working well and you have a plan for replacing facilities as they no longer become effective at the end of their life. However, most organisations do not have a clearly defined plan for replacing existing facilities, so it may be beneficial to start recording digital data as you undertake significant refurbishment or repurposing of existing facilities.

For example, if you have a large multistorey building, you may have a plan for refurbishing the facility floor by floor over a period of many years. By collecting the as-built digital data of each floor as its refurbished, you will eventually piece together the the digital data of the facility to provide a useful and full working model. This is one situation where the use of point cloud surveys, or digital surveys, will provide definite benefits. Your digital model would be developed using digital survey information, providing you with accurate and reliable data.

It can be really useful to obtain the digital cloud point survey before you start designing the new layouts. This way you can be sure that your design will accurately fit within your existing floor plate. As your design and installation progresses new information will be added to the baseline that's provided by the point cloud survey.

This general approach can apply to any existing facility that does not currently have digital model data. Even if you don't have a plan to refurbish the whole of a facility, it's likely that over time you will have modelled and obtained data for significant volumes of existing buildings. As a building reaches a position where a significant proportion has accurate digital data, the strategic decision to complete the data by filling in the missing parts becomes easier to make.

All of this information should be recorded within your Organisation Information Requirement (OIR), which provides the overarching details of how your data will be managed. Significant projects should always have a project specific EIR, which will follow the details and processes within your OIR and will be supplemented with project specific information.

DATA MAINTENANCE PLAN

To ensure that any regular or ongoing task takes place it's useful to have a plan. This also applies to the maintenance of your data.

All of the above items, responsibilities, data validation and ongoing maintenance should be included within your plan. This should make sure you know how often data should be validated, how data should be updated and the way each task should be done.

The plan will become a valuable point of reference, so anyone within your team should be able to understand the data requirements allowing seamless transfer of responsibilities.

You also need to consider how often the plan will be reviewed and updated. BIM and the related estates data will continue to evolve and adapt, so you need to be sure that any evolutionary effects on your systems are incorporated into your plan. It's ideal to have a six-monthly interim review with the intention of a full review every year.

TRUST IN YOUR DATA

If you haven't validated your model or you haven't maintained your data, then trust will be lost in your model the first time someone encounters incorrect information. If errors and incorrect information are found on a regular basis then eventually the trust in the model will become so low that the model will not get used. All the time, effort and cost invested into developing your model will become wasted. Of course this is an extreme example, you will have opportunities in the early days of using your model to correct the errors and prevent your model from becoming obsolete, but without timely corrections there is high risk of your data becoming useless.

The trust also applies to maintaining your data. If you don't maintain your data the information contained within will eventually become outdated and irrelevant. If someone refers to the model and finds incorrect information, once again, trust will be lost.

FUTURE-PROOFING YOUR DATA

A particularly divisive question that often gets polarised views is the best approach to future-proofing your model and your data.

We have three specific areas here:

1. The file and data formats.
2. Predicting future data uses.
3. Data as an enabler for future facility uses.

The one aspect that has become widely accepted is the use of the open IFC format from buildingSMART for your model. This is likely to ensure that your data remains relevant in a file format that can be accessed whatever new systems or software are used in the future. IFC at its core is just a text file that can be read with any text reader - the file can be read with Microsoft Word, various plain text readers and even in the Chrome web browser.

It's quite impenetrable to understand the meaning of the contents of an IFC file by using a text viewer, but the point is that the file can be read at a very basic level, without requiring expensive or specific software applications. Unlike commercial file formats that are locked down requiring commercial applications to make any sense of the information contained within the file.

But, how about the specific information that you require to be contained within your model? Can this be employed to future-proof the model and extend its usability?

This is where I firmly believe that it's a near impossible task to predict the future. If you are trying to future-proof the data within the model by predicting what uses you will have for the data in the future, your decisions are not likely to be the correct ones. The measurement and definition of the information many change, at one time in the UK we rated boilers using British Thermal Units, for example, but now we use kilowatts.

We also return to the cost of collecting and maintaining data that isn't being used, which is a wasteful exercise. If you can't predict the future then don't attempt to future-proof your model by adding layers of data that you don't know if you have a specific use for.

This doesn't apply if you have a specific plan and roadmap for implementing new tools that require specific items of data. You may have a plan to start using a new system for managing space utilisation and this requires occupant numbers for each room. Your existing systems cannot use this data, but you know the new system will require the data. This is a completely different scenario, as you are not attempting to predict a future, instead you are planning for a known new data requirement.

The final aspect of future-proofing is having data within your model to enable you to make informed decisions about the how spaces or the facility as a whole can be used or changed for new purposes. This way of approaching future-proofing does not ask you to predict the future. In a way it does the opposite. It accepts that we cannot possibly put measures in place that would allow for all future uses. Instead we provide a baseline of data that makes it easier to understand how spaces and facilities can be repurposed.

By providing data that quantifies the number of occupants that can be accommodated in a space, you will know whether another workstation can be added without affecting the quality of fresh air. Or whether the allowable floor loadings will allow a space to be altered from storage space to an occupied space.

It's easy to fall into the trap of requesting all possible data to enable all possible future repurposing options to be assessed. Instead, consider the data that is really critical or useful in making such decisions. Once again, too much data will not be cost-effective and will require maintaining.

CHAPTER SUMMARY

Data devalues over time. The only way to reduce this decline in value is to expend money to maintain your asset (your data).

- Validate your project model at each of the design stages.
- The more data you have within a model, the greater the task in maintaining the data. It's wasteful to maintain data that you don't use.
- Validating your data is a technical and objective exercise. It involves analysing the data for omissions and errors.
- Ongoing maintenance - develop a plan for minor and major updates to your data and to your model.
- You need to have trust and confidence in your data, this is achieved by validating and maintaining your data.
- Future-proof your data through the use of the buildingSMART IFC file format.

CHAPTER 11: EMPLOYER'S INFORMATION REQUIREMENTS (EIR)

Employer's Information Requirements (EIR) - A pre-tender document that sets out the information to be delivered, and the standards and processes to be adopted by the supplier as part of the project delivery process.
(PAS 1192-2:2013)

YOUR PROJECT EIR

Your Employer's Information Requirements (EIR) are the number one important documents to have in place for any BIM project. You will lose out on those crucially important BIM deliverables if you do not have a project EIR.

WHAT IS EIR?

> An EIR provides clear guidance on your BIM requirements for your project. It details exactly what the BIM deliverables will be, when they will be provided and who will provide them.

It also details other aspects of BIM management and processes that you require for your project, such as your file-naming protocol, file formats and the project Common Data Environment (CDE).

PAS 1192-2 - Specification for information management for the capital/delivery phase of construction projects using building information modelling provides a schedule of what should be included within an EIR, as detailed below.

However, its schedule should be seen as an initial reference point for what may be included within your EIR. If an item isn't applicable to you, then don't add pointless and unnecessary information to your EIR. The content of your EIR should detail all your requirements and no more. It should be as concise as possible. These documents can be complicated enough by just including the information that is important to you. Why would you want to risk your key requirements being misinterpreted, ignored or potentially introducing contradictory information by adding superfluous stuff?

To make sure your EIR is as concise as possible, appraise your content. Does it:

- Include enough information and detail for your requirements to be understood, and exclude information that is surplus to your requirements?
- Include only information that is relevant and beneficial for the intended purpose?
- Avoid ambiguous requirements?

WHY AN EIR?

You need to provide clear guidance to your team. This applies for every aspect of a project. Your design brief needs to be clear and unambiguous, as do your data requirements.

In the early days of BIM we had project briefs and specifications which simply stated that a project required BIM Level 2. At the very best, such a statement identifies a minimum level of BIM that should be provided for a project, federated models and data deliverables. At the other end of the scale, a BIM Level 2 statement doesn't clarify how detailed the federated models should be, or what data is required. So a couple of concept models with a minimal amount of data could (available through a CDE) could be the outcome of such a statement.

We have moved a long way from such blanket statements. Knowledge and understanding within the industry has improved immensely.

> I think that most clients and employers' agents are now aware that a BIM project requires an EIR. And, certainly, designers and main contractors immediately want to understand exactly what is required if they hear BIM mentioned.

An EIR is different and separate to an employer's requirement, which focuses on the requirements of the physical facility. An EIR focuses on the requirements of the digital version of the physical facility.

An employer's requirement does not provided much detail of the information that an employer will want from a project beyond generic requirements such as operating and maintenance manuals, or as-built information. An employer's requirement generally focuses on the requirements of the physical facility. In time, the two documents could potentially become integrated into a single employer's requirement, but for now, a BIM project will need both an employer's requirement and an EIR - employer's information requirements.

As the name suggests, an effective EIR needs to provide clear guidance on the information an employer requires. There should also be an effort to avoid conflict with the information requirements of other project documents. Any legacy information requirements that belong to the legacy of an employer's requirement - but would sit more comfortably within the EIR - should be moved across to the EIR to avoid potential confusion.

> Without an EIR, it's very unlikely that you will receive the information that you require.

Most project disputes tend to arise from insufficient clarity. A comprehensive EIR removes risk due to a lack of clarity. It makes sure all your stakeholders understand their responsibilities for the delivery of project information.

THE CONTENT OF AN EIR

The requirements of an EIR according to the BIM Level 2 document, *PAS 1192-2 the Specification for information management for the capital/delivery phase of construction projects using building information modelling*, is separated into three main areas: Information Management; Commercial Management; and Competence Assessment. These three main sections are broken down as follows:

Information Management

1. Levels of detail (LOD).
2. Training requirements.
3. Planning of work and data segregation.
4. Coordination and clash detection.
5. Collaboration process.
6. Health and Safety Executive (HSE) / Construction Design Management (CDM) regulations.
7. A schedule of security and integrity requirements for the project.
8. A schedule of specific information to be excluded or included from information models.
9. A schedule of constraints set by the employer on the size of model files, the size of extranet uploads or emails, or the file formats that can define the size of a volume.
10. Compliance plan - requirements for bidders' proposals for the management of the coordination process.
11. A definition of any 3D coordinate origin/system required by the employer to place graphical models.
12. A schedule of any software formats, including version numbers, that will be used by organisations or individuals in the supply chain to deliver the project.

Commercial Management

1. Exchange of information - alignment of information exchanges, work stages, purpose and required formats.
2. Client's strategic purposes - details of the expected purposes for information provided in models.
3. A schedule of any software formats, including version numbers, that will be used by organisations or individuals in the supply chain to deliver the project.
4. An initial responsibility matrix setting out any discipline responsibilities for model or information production in line with the defined project stages.
5. A schedule of the standards and guidance documents.
6. A schedule of any changes to the standard competencies set out in the contract.

Competence Assessment

1. Details of the competence assessment that bidders must respond to.
2. Changes to associated tender documentation.
3. BIM tender assessment details.

I will provide some clarity on each of the above sections, but remember it is unlikely that every section will apply to your project. It's all too common for generic and irrelevant information to be provided for each of the above sections even when it does not apply to a project. Every section should be considered for each new project and included within your EIR if the content will benefit your project.

INFORMATION MANAGEMENT

1: LEVELS OF DETAIL (LOD)

Chapter 6: Model checking expands on levels of detail (LOD) in the graphical elements of your model.

The detail contained in your model will increase over time, and different suppliers will be responsible for providing different elements of your model.

You need to consider how you inform your suppliers what LOD should be applied to your model?

There are three distinct parts to LOD:

- How LOD will be measured.
- What the LOD should be at each stage of a project.
- And who will be responsible for providing the required LOD.

The easiest and simplest way to define how LOD will be measured is to reference an established measurement method.

At BIMsense, we generally reference the NBS BIM toolkit for LOD. The NBS toolkit provides LOD measurement from LOD2 (the lowest level of detail provided on the NBS toolkit) through to LOD5 (the highest level of detail provided on NBS toolkit) for a wide range of asset types. One benefit of the NBS BIM toolkit is that its LOD definitions are referenced to Uniclass 2015 codes. There isn't an LOD definition for all the thousands of Uniclass codes, but it is a useful way of defining LOD.

For asset types that are not contained within the toolkit, but are critical to your organisation, you can provide your own definitions. Otherwise, you can make it clear that reference should be made to similar assets that are defined. This isn't a fully objective and measurable approach, but it should be suitable for non-critical asset types.

You will also be able to learn from your projects if you encounter problematic asset types that require defining, as you will be able to add your own definitions to future projects.

An alternative LOD definition can be obtained from the BIMforum level of development specification. Unlike the NBS toolkit approach, this provides a document approach to defining LOD, but it is very comprehensive. It uses a different measurement scale for LOD: LOD100, LOD200, LOD300, LOD350 and LOD400.

As for the other two items what the LOD should be at each stage of a project and who will be responsible for providing the required LOD, these are best referenced through a model production and delivery table (MPDT), which is detailed within the section 'An initial responsibility matrix setting out any discipline responsibilities for model or information production in line with the defined project stages' later in this chapter.

2: TRAINING REQUIREMENTS

I can't imagine that many projects will need you to include training requirements, unless you need your CDE to be set up and hosted by your lead designer.

This section shouldn't be used for identifying the training needs of your supply chain, as this should be identified through BIM competency unless you have a bespoke requirement to train your supply chain.

If this section isn't applicable, don't provide a paragraph of irrelevant text. Keep it simple and identify the fact that you do not require any employer-specific training.

3: PLANNING OF WORK AND DATA SEGREGATION

This is an important section. It establishes some of the basic requirements for your project information.

PAS 1192-2 provides additional clarity for this section: *Requirements for bidder's proposals for the management of the modelling process (e.g model management, naming conventions, etc).*

In addition to the above, it is beneficial to you as an employer to have some control over these requirements.

It is really beneficial for your organisation to develop its own file-naming protocol. It will ensure that all the files you receive are aligned with your protocol. This will enable you to navigate and locate information in an efficient way. It makes sense that the naming protocol for a project is aligned with the end-user requirements. As an estate manager, you will be accessing the project information for much longer than just the design and construction period.

Ideally, you should follow the file-naming convention as detailed within *BS 1192*, the code of practice for collaborative working process, and extended within *PAS 1192-2*.

Following the details in the guidance documents is the easiest way to gain compliance from your suppliers, as any supplier who can deliver BIM Level 2 should already be following the *BS 1192* file-naming convention.

Other benefits to following the BIM Level 2 standard file-naming conventions include: automatic validation of file naming by many CDEs; faster location and identification of your information; familiarity of the file-naming convention across organisations; and the possibility of setting up automated checking of information based on the fact that you know exactly how a document will named, before it is created.

File naming is just one part of this particular section. Another interlinked requirement deals with model management. This details how a model will be separated, how it may link with existing, or legacy, models and the reference numbers of the different models. Model volumes, which allow you to separate large models, provide some clarity for model management.

A model volume reference is included within the standard file name, so, let's look at file naming in more detail. The BIM Level 2 file-naming convention separates the file name into sections, each sections with its own code that provides a unique piece of information.

The file naming codes consist of various sections each separated by a hyphen:

Project - Originator - Volume or System - Level and Location - Type - Role - Classification - Number - Suitability - Revision - File Extension Suffix

This will provide a very long and initially complex file name. However, some of the sections are optional. *Classification* is an optional section, and I have yet to come across a project that requires a classification code within the file name. So let's assume that a classification code will not be required. *Suitability* and *Revision* codes are required, but only if your CDE does not provide this information in another way. Most commercial CDEs require all uploaded documents to be given a suitability (or status) code and a revision during the upload process. If your CDE has this function - and most do - then you will not require *Suitability* and *Revision* codes in the file name. The file extension suffix, such as .pdf and .ifc almost always occurs without manual input during the process of generating files. So we will also ignore this part of the file name.

This leaves the file name for most projects as:

Project - Originator - Volume or System - Level and Location - Type - Role - Number

This is much easier to navigate and understand. A typical architectural model could be named as:

HICC-MA-11-ZZ-M3-A-0001

Some sections are relatively easy to understand, some are a little more difficult. Let's look at each of the remaining file-naming sections and what you will require within your EIR.

PROJECT

This is a reference for your project. Ideally, this should be generated within your organisation. This will then be the reference that is added to the start of all project files and should remain with all files throughout the life of the asset.

It's much better for you to be in control of this reference rather than something being produced by your lead designer that doesn't fully align with your needs. Or, even worse, each of your designers provide their own project reference.

Your EIR should simply state the project reference and that it should be used in all file naming. You may also decide to use the project reference within other information such as correspondence.

To align with *BS 1192*, this code should be from two to six characters. But, as with all guidance, if there is a specific reason that you can justify why you require additional characters then you should use codes that work for you.

If you have multiple projects or lots of smaller projects you may want to separate the project code with additional references. Say your overall project has reference *HICC*, you could reference the smaller projects or sub-projects as *HICC1, HICC2* and so on. Alternatively, you could reference smaller projects through the volume code.

ORIGINATOR

This section provides a unique reference for each supplier that provides information. It doesn't just have to be design information, it could be any project information. When I say a unique reference, it only needs to be unique for your project, although there will be future benefits if each of your suppliers across past, present and future projects has its own reference. This will enable you to instantly access to all the information ever produced by each supplier.

Originator codes should be between three and six characters, to comply with *BS 1192*. However you're unlikely to need more than three characters to provide a unique reference, and this keeps your file reference concise. Using letters alone gives you more than 17,000 unique letter combinations. Using numbers as well as letters gives you more than 45,000 combinations and, if you really want to, you could also add special characters.

When assigning organisational codes I find that it helps if each organisation suggests its preferred code. Most designers will have a code that they would prefer to use.

When it comes to your EIR, at the very start of a project it's unlikely that you will be able to assign any external organisational codes and you certainly won't be able to assign all codes to all the organisations that will be involved in your project. Therefore, you need to provide the rules for the organisational codes: how many characters they should be, the format (numbers, letters etc), and whether the codes will require your acceptance.

Ideally, let your lead designer manage the organisational codes at the start of a project, and your main contractor later in the project. If required, you can ask them to obtain approval for each code.

VOLUME OR SYSTEM

The Volume or System code is often the most confused and least understood section of standard file naming.

It doesn't help that the code can be used for two different identification purposes. It can be used to identify a volume or a system.

Let's first look at what a system is and how the code can be used to identify a system. Systems are a common way of describing and grouping the different parts of a facility. Within the Uniclass 2015 classifications we have a whole table entirely for different systems associated with a facility. Building services, such as the mechanical ventilation or the low temperature hot water for heating, are commonly grouped and described as systems. But, if you take a look at the Uniclass 2015 Ss-Systems table you will see that it lists many other systems such as a curtain walling system or a structural slab system.

This means we can use a code to identify the system that an item of information represents. It helps us to easily understand what information is contained within a drawing, a schedule, a model or any other document.

You may also think that it would then make sense that we would use the Uniclass system codes for the system code within the file name. But *BS 1192*, which provides the standard file-naming guidance, details that the volume or system code should be one or two characters. A Uniclass 2015 system code could be as many as 14 characters, which probably wouldn't be suitable for use within the file naming.

In addition, *BS 1192* does not provide any recommendations for system codes (it only provides a single recommendation for a volume code). This suggests that system codes should be project-specific. In some ways this is beneficial. It's unlikely that each file would only contain a single Uniclass system, it's more likely that files will contain a combination of closely related systems. This makes it easier to develop a method of identifying a combination of systems without requiring a very long arrangement of codes within the file name.

You could, for example, have a code for all the mechanical building services or all the small power and data.

In Chapter 8: Classifications, we looked at the different classification systems that have been used in construction. The CI/SfB (the Construction Index/Samarbetskommitten for Byggnadsfragor) classification system still remains familiar to many construction professionals.

As an example, the following codes (based on CI/SfB) could be used for your system codes within your standard file naming:

XX Not applicable to the codes below
00 Information contains multiple systems

Building systems

01 GA Plans

02 GA Elevations

03 GA Sections

04 Visualizations

06 Acoustics

08 Health and Safety

09 Fire strategy

Substructure

11 Groundworks

13 Floor beds, ground floors, basements

16 Foundations, retaining walls

17 Pile foundations

Structure

20 Detail location

21 External walls

22 Internal walls, partitions

23 Floors, including beams

24 Stairs

27 Roofs, including beams

28 Building frames

29 Patent glazing

31 External wall openings

32 Internal wall openings

33 Access floors

34 Balustrades

35 Suspended ceilings

37 Roof openings

Finishes

41 Wall finishes: external

42 Wall finishes: internal

43 Floor finishes

44 Stair finishes

45 Ceiling finishes

47 Roof finishes

Services

50 Mechanical schematics

52 Drainage

53 Hot and cold water

54 Gas, air and steam

56 Space heating

57 Air conditioning, ventilation

59 Flues, fuel storage, etc.

60 Electrical schematics

61 Electrical mains and standby supply

62 Electrical power circuits and accessories

63 Lighting

64 Communications

66 Transport: lifts, escalators, conveyors etc.

67 Fire alarm

68 Security

Fittings

70 Room elevations

71 Circulation fittings, signs, etc.

72 Furniture and accessories

73 Catering services and kitchen units

74 Sanitary and bathroom fittings

75 Cleaning and laundry fittings

76 Storage, cloakroom fittings

77 Special fittings

78 Soft furnishings and upholstery

External works

90 External works

91 Site information

92 Survey information

It needs to pointed out that the use of the above codes wouldn't necessarily provide a fully efficient method of referencing your system. It references a legacy classification system which is now largely unused because it failed to meet the current needs of the construction industry. However, it could aid understanding of information, which would provide benefits.

The other use of this part of the standard file naming is to identify volumes. Volumes, unlike systems, do not look at closely related building elements, instead they look at distinct parts of a project. A whole new facility could be a volume. If you had an existing building that needed an extension, the existing building could be one volume and the extension another. If a project consisted of three interconnected buildings you could identify each building as a separate volume.

It's worth considering the purpose of separating a project into volumes. The main reason for using well-defined volumes is to help with managing project models. For large and complex models, the file size of design models can become very large, in excess of 500MB. The size of such models will mean that downloading, accessing, querying and validating the models will take more time than with a model half the size. This can be especially problematic during the construction phase, when models tend to be at their largest size, because data continues to be added to models during each project stage until completion. At completion, any non-useful information should be removed before handover. During the construction phase, we also see data links that are not as good as those during the earlier stages, as temporary building sites tend to be more dependent on mobile internet networks.

Volumes can assist in the overall management of your information, as you may find it beneficial to separate a large project into more manageable chunks.

Like system codes, *BS 1192* doesn't prescribe the codes that should be used for volumes.

BS 1192 lists ZZ for all volumes. It also very common to use XX where a volume does not apply, this is particularly relevant for general non-design type documentation where you require standard file naming. The use of XX comes from the extension of the *BS 1192* codes for levels and location. XX within levels and locations is used when there is *no level applicable*.

Therefore, volume codes should also be project specific. If you adopt the CI/SfB codes for systems, then you will need a method of identifying volumes that distinguishes it as a volume code and not a system code. For example, you could use only letters, or a combination of letters and numbers (below, n represents a numerical digit 0-9):

An - Existing volumes

Bn - New building volumes

Cn - External volumes

This can be further adapted to your particular needs. If you manage a large estate with multiple sites, you can identify each site with its own reference.

It's worth spending some time to carefully consider how the volume and system codes can be adapted to help make it easier to access your information during the projects and during the lifetime of your facility. The time invested here could easily save your organisation that time multiplied manifold during the life of your facility by enabling simple, quick and effective access to your data.

One thing that will need to be defined if you plan to use both volume and system codes is that when naming a file you will only be able to use one code. For example, if you have an external model volume that contains only external works information, you could have a 90 system code or a C0 volume code. It is normal for 3D models to be identified by a volume code and for other information to be identified by a system code.

LEVELS AND LOCATIONS

This is a nice, simple part of standard file naming. It enables information to be separated and identified by the level to which it applies.

BS 1192 provides the following codes:

ZZ - Multiple levels

XX - No levels applicable

GF - Ground floor

00 - Base level of building (where ground floor is not applicable)

01 - Floor 1

02 - Floor 2

M1 - Mezzanine above level 01

M2 - Mezzanine above level 02

B1 - Level 1 below ground floor

B2 - Level 2 below ground floor

PAS 1192-2 also provides some additional information for file naming, although not as comprehensive as BS 1192, which adds the following to the available codes:

LG1 - Lower ground floor level 1

There are a couple of items that require a closer look. The use of GF for the ground level (and B1 for basement 1 and M1 for mezzanine above level 1) of a building, within file naming will mean that files will not list in a fully logical and useful way. Take an example:

HICC-AG-62-01-DR-E-2101 - First floor containment

HICC-AG-62-02-DR-E-2102 - Second floor containment

HICC-AG-62-GF-DR-E-2100 - Ground floor containment

By using GF as a level code, the ground floor containment will usually be listed (if sorted by file name) after the upper levels. However, if we were to use 00 as the code for the ground floor level, the listing of files becomes easier to navigate:

HICC-AG-62-00-DR-E-2100 - Ground floor containment

HICC-AG-62-01-DR-E-2101 - First floor containment

HICC-AG-62-02-DR-E-2102 - Second floor containment

This results in ground floor being listed before the upper levels.

The standard codes do not have a reference for roof levels. It often helps with clarity if an open roof level is not listed as a level code. The prefix R can be used for roof codes. Another consideration with roofs is the situation where you have a less conventional building with multiple roofs at multiple levels. In such a scenario, you may want the roof code to relate to the level code. For example R2 could be a section of roof that is accessed from level 02.

If you have a current established system for level codes you may want to continue with your current system. It's also clear from the example file name within *PAS 1192-2* (*section 9.3.2*) which has an *LG1* reference that the level code is not limited to two characters.

To sum up, ideally follow the guidelines of *BS 1192* for levels and locations. But, as the *BS 1192* guidance doesn't cover every possible scenario, the level and location codes should work for your unique organisational and project needs. It should also be flexible enough to work for your future project requirements.

TYPE

Type codes provide a reference to the type of information contained within a file. This could be to identify that the file is a 3D model, a schedule or a drawing.

Ideally, it's useful to follow the type codes guidance within *BS 1192*:

File types for drawings and models:

AF - Animation file (of a model)

CM - Combined model - this is also referred to as a federated model

CR - Specific for the clash process

DR - 2D drawing

M2 - 2D model file

M3 - 3D model file

MR - Model rendition file for other renditions, for example, thermal analysis

VS - Visualisations

File types for documents:

BQ - Bill of quantities

CA - Calculations

CO - Correspondence

CP - Cost plan

DB - Database

FN - File note

HS - Health and safety

IE - Information exchange file

MI - Minutes / action notes

MS - Method statement

PP - Presentation

PR - Programme

RD - Room data sheet

RI - Request for information

RP - Report

SA - Schedule of information

SH - Schedule

SN - Snagging list

SP - Specification

SU - Survey

Many of the above codes are very clear on when they should be used, others are not so clear. The health and safety code is particularly interesting. It's hard to imagine anything produced for health and safety that wouldn't also apply to another type code. For example, a drawing that indicated emergency escape routes could have the HS code and could also be referenced as a 2D drawing (DR). A document that identifies emergency procedures could have the HS code and also the method statement code (MS). And what is the difference between a schedule and a schedule of information, all schedules contain information? But, with addition clarification we could easily identify that a schedule of information lists out other files.

It's useful to also have an XX code for files that do not contain information that can be referenced.

Interestingly, the type code also has a closely related Uniclass 2015 table, the PM - Project Management table. This contains 387 codes that can be applied to types of information. Clearly, we don't want such complexity within our file-naming type codes. But, for additional clarity it may be useful to reference each of the file-naming type codes for a project against each of the applicable Uniclass PM codes.

Once again, you want to have codes that work for your organisation and your projects. Consider all the possibilities and develop a well-defined and robust schedule of codes.

ROLE

Role codes describe the role that an organisation fulfills. A multidisciplinary organisation may have more than one role in a single project, or across multiple projects.

BS 1192 describes that role codes should be just one character. This could provide limitations, depending how detailed you require the allocated roles to be. The Uniclass 2015 PM - Project Management table has more than 100 different role classifications. But, similar to the type codes, to aid simplicity it's possible to allocate multiple Uniclass codes to a single file-naming role code character.

The role codes scheduled within *BS 1192*:

A - Architect

B - Building surveyor

C - Civil engineer

D - Drainage, highways engineer

E - Electrical engineer

F - Facilities management

G - Geographical and land surveyor

H - Heating and ventilation designer

I - Interior designer

K - Client

L - Landscape architect

M - Mechanical engineer

P - Public health engineer

Q - Quantity surveyor

S - Structural engineer

T - Town and country planner

W - Contractor

X - Subcontractor

Y - Specialist designer

Z - General (non-disciplinary)

The guidance also helpfully lists the characters J, N, R, U and V for non-standard project-specific roles. It also states that project-specific codes with more than two characters can also be used.

NUMBER

Quite a simple one, this is the number code within a file name. It's just a sequential number.

> BS 1192 identifies that the number should consist of four digits. Although, the example file name within PAS 1192-2 consists of five digits.

PAS 1192-2 also identifies that number is unique when linked with file type (the type code) and discipline (the role code). So this could mean that you could have multiple files with the number 0001. But, when combined with type and role the combined reference will be unique:

...-M3-A-0001

...-DR-A-0001

So the above extracted codes would both be produced by the architectural team with a number 0001, but the ...*M3-A-0001* would describe a 3D model, and the ...*DR-A-0001* would describe a drawing.

> The main thing when developing your file naming is that your consider your full organisational needs (your immediate needs and your possible future needs), and that you document in a clear and concise way your requirements, preventing ambiguous and conflicting information where possible.

MODEL MANAGEMENT

I'm of the opinion that a good proportion of model management is dealt with through standard file naming, especially the consideration of project volumes.

The detail of your data requirements, including attribute naming, should be provided in full as an appendix to your EIR. Depending on the extent of your data requirements, this information may need to be provided in an electronic format.

As part of model management you may also want to detail your requirements on the layers and the layer naming, which is similar to file naming and detailed within BS 1192. However, unless you have a specific need for a particular format, this is usually best left to your designers. After all, we are not looking to remove the responsibility of design from our designers, we are just looking to receive the design information in a specific format that provides us with additional benefits.

4: COORDINATION AND CLASH DETECTION

This is another important section. It should explain: your minimum expectations for the quality of the model; what checks are required; and where responsibility lies for those checks. It will be relatively generic as most of your projects will require the same level of model quality. So once set up, you just need to review it to check that the information remains relevant.

We have a whole chapter for model checking. This part of the EIR specifically refers to the graphical model.

Model checking and clash detection should be done by each organisation that produces design models. Each originator is responsible for ensuring that their own model, in isolation, non-federated, is free of clashes. If you have a single building services designer, the building services model should be free of clashes. The ventilation should not clash with the electrical containment or the cold water supply. All of this is common sense, however it needs to be explicitly identified, it's always surprising the number of projects that do not have clash-free single-discipline models.

The federated model is a little more complicated, especially when it comes to establishing the responsibility for the checking. Ultimately, you will want a coordinated and clash-free federated model. Clash-free and coordinated single discipline models are fantastic, but it's the whole project model (the federated model) that needs to be clash-free and coordinated. There's little benefit with a federated model that has hundreds of clashes between steelwork and building services. It just will not provide you with a model that represents your physical asset. The clashes that occur in your model will be resolved during the construction process, but unless it is updated, the model will not represent the completed facility.

You need to identify clear responsibilities for model checking and coordinating the federated model. This natural fit is for your lead designer to take on this role. Lead designers should have a general responsibility for coordinating the design, and this should include the federated model. But, if you don't explicitly state where responsibility lies, this doesn't always happen.

If your lead designer is unable to do this, the alternative approach is to give this role to a separate organisation. While this approach has an advantage in that it gives you an independent assessment of the model, your first solution should remain with your lead designer.

So, what do you need to have within your EIR? It's useful to explicitly identify the following:

- Single-discipline models should be free from clashes before being shared. It's acceptable for work in progress (WIP) models to have clashes, but models should be checked before they are uploaded to your CDE to ensure that clashes are eliminated.

- Responsibility for checking the federated model.

- You may want to detail the format and the nature of the checking. At BIMsense, we always provide our model issues in the BIM Collaboration Format (BCF).

- The model should reflect the completed asset. For this to occur, the design should be buildable and complete. If a model has internal walls that need to finish at the soffit of the above slab, but details them finishing short of the soffit, then the model will not represent the completed asset.

- The model should also be suitable for your data requirements. As an example, internal partition walls may require fire ratings. For your data to be correct, walls will need to be separated into distinct sections. Walls surrounding a kitchen will form a fire compartment and you need to ensure that this rating is only applied to the applicable walls and doesn't extend to sections of walls that do not form the compartment.

- You should also include any modelling requirements that are specific to your organisation.

The method of communicating this information (your CDE) and the frequency of checking should be identified in the next section, collaboration process.

5: COLLABORATION PROCESS

The amount of control you need for your project will depend upon the amount of information in this section. You may want to leave the day-to-day design to your designers and the day-to-day construction to your contractor, which means you can ask for information to be provided at the completion of stages, which will be scheduled within the information exchanges section.

If you want to take the hands-off approach, then leave the collaboration process to your designers and just make sure the process is effectively managed. Ask for the collaboration process your team will follow to be detailed before appointment within the pre-contract BIM Execution Plan. This will also provide you with the tools to check that members of your team are doing what they said they would.

This could also include the project CDE. The ideal scenario is one in which you have your own organisational CDE, where project information is uploaded. If this is not possible, you need to make sure someone is responsible for providing and managing the project CDE. Once again, this responsibility can be given to your suppliers, usually either the lead designer or the project manager.

Alternatively, you may want full access to the developing information during the design and construction phases.

This will give you a higher level of transparency and accountability. Your organisational CDE becomes the central source of information for your project. You then provide the process for uploading information, i.e. where information should be uploaded to. When it comes to the project models, you also detail how often these should be checked and uploaded.

EIRs often schedule the BIM-specific meetings that revolve around the model checks and uploads for a project. However, it can often be sufficient to require that model quality and model coordination is made an integral part of existing project meetings, such as design team meetings.

6: HEALTH AND SAFETY EXECUTIVE (HSE) / CONSTRUCTION DESIGN MANAGEMENT (CDM) REGULATIONS

Within most EIRs, this is one area where it is difficult to justify including a dedicated section to health and safety and construction design management (CDM). Before you throw your arms up and shout that health and safety is the number one priority, I'm not suggesting that health and safety isn't the most important item of any project, it is, and it always will be. However, the document that we are looking at is the EIR, the employer's information requirements.

Most EIRs provide a section for health and safety, with a paragraph of text that explains designers' CDM responsibilities. I struggle to see the relevance of including this information within an EIR. Competent designers will be fully aware of their duties under the CDM regulations and a designer's overall competency should be assessed before any appointment is made, as required by the CDM regulations. It's almost as if we don't have the ability to relate health and safety to the project information requirements, so to avoid any accusations of not taking health and safety seriously, we add some text to make a designer aware of their CDM responsibilities.

On the flipside, if you do require specific health and safety information then this is the place to include it. You may require health and safety data within your model to identify residual risks by using the either *IFC Pset_Risk* the *PAS 1192-6 HS_Risk_UK* property sets. Such information would absolutely justify having this section, and the specifics of what you require.

You may also want your model to be checked for common risks and for these risks to be identified as BCF issues. An example of such a risk would be maintainable services that are located above a specified height above slab level. Having services that require maintenance at high level, for example in a double-height atrium space, would require access equipment such as a mobile scaffold tower, which introduces avoidable risks to a facility.

So, in your EIR, include specific data and information requirements that will allow you to assess and reduce health and safety risks and to enable all your designers to fulfill their CDM responsibilities. But, do not use this section to explain your designers' CDM duties.

7: A SCHEDULE OF ANY SECURITY AND INTEGRITY REQUIREMENTS FOR THE PROJECT

This section is similar to the previous section on HSE/CDM requirements. If your project has specific security needs, then this is the section to detail those requirements. But don't feel that you have to pad out a section because you have don't have anything relevant to add. Remember we want our EIR to be as useful as possible, so you should always only include information if it is relevant and providing some benefit.

Any organisation-specific security requirements relating to the project information should be included within this section.

Even if you believe you do not have any project-specific security requirements for your information, you should always provide the project with a security assessment classification.

PAS 1192-5 the specification for security-minded building information modelling, digital built environments and smart asset management details how you can assess the security classification of your project. Your security classification will consist of a rating from S1 (the highest security rating) to S4 (the lowest security rating). For projects with an S4 classification, no further action will be required apart from confirming the rating within your EIR and adding any organisation-specific requirements that you may have.

Ratings S1 to S3 will require you to include additional information, such as security protocols and plans for managing a security breach. For an S1 project, you may have professionals for managing your project's security.

8: A SCHEDULE OF ANY SPECIFIC INFORMATION TO BE EITHER EXCLUDED OR INCLUDED FROM INFORMATION MODELS

A bit of a strange section, this. The details of information to be included within your model should be identified through your model production and delivery table (MPDT). And the most common scenario for excluding information from your model arises when you have a S1 or S2 security classification that asks you not to include certain sensitive information. For example, you may want covert security cameras to be included within your model. But, for me, it makes more sense for the schedule of security-sensitive information to be excluded from your model, and included within the Information Management section 7: A schedule of any security and integrity requirements for the project.

In reality, you are unlikely to need to add anything to this section. However, if you have specific requirements that should be included or excluded from your model (with the exception of security-sensitive items) then this is the place. But, remember, keep them concise and relevant.

9: A SCHEDULE OF ANY PARTICULAR CONSTRAINTS SET BY THE EMPLOYER ON THE SIZE OF MODEL FILES, THE SIZE OF EXTRANET UPLOADS OR EMAILS, OR THE FILE FORMATS THAT CAN DEFINE THE SIZE OF A VOLUME

Model volumes have been discussed within the above planning of work and data segregation and standard file-naming requirements sections. If you have a specific reason for limiting the size of your model, then this is clearly the place where you should provide this information. This could be due to technical reasons, such as limitations from your CDE.

However, if you believe you may have a problem within large model files, possibly due to a large and complex project, then it is a better approach to identify the model volumes and model systems that you will require at the start of your project.

If you were to just provide a maximum size of model file, then you leave the decision of separating you project into volumes to your model originators. The arbitrary model volumes may be useful to your designers, but they are unlikely to be consistent between designers and unlikely to provide you with other model management benefits.

This section also references the maximum size of emails and other file types. Email attachments should never be problem as all your project information should be contained within the CDE, and emails are a poor substitute for collaboration. If you have restrictions on the maximum size of file types, these restrictions should be identified here, ideally in a clear and understandable schedule.

10: COMPLIANCE PLAN - REQUIREMENTS FOR BIDDERS' PROPOSALS FOR THE MANAGEMENT OF THE COORDINATION PROCESS

This is simple one. A compliance plan should be provided at the time of tender through the submission of a pre-contract BIM Execution Plan (BEP). The information to be included within the pre-contract BEP is defined and scheduled within *PAS 1192-2*.

You should have a pre-contract BEP prior to the appointment of your design team, with the pre-contract BEP provided by your lead designer as part of their tender process, and ideally coordinated with the other designers. You should also have a pre-contract BEP prior to the appointment of your construction delivery team, and always for projects where design responsibilities transfer to the main contractor.

Any information identified within *PAS 1192-2* as being required within a pre-contract BEP, but that is not required for your project, should be identified within this section. This will help your bidders to focus on providing relevant information.

11: A DEFINITION OF ANY COORDINATE ORIGIN/SYSTEM (3D) THAT THE EMPLOYER REQUIRES TO BE USED TO PLACE GRAPHICAL MODELS

You will want your model to be located according to real-world coordinates. For the purpose of clarity within this section, coordinates will also include elevation information. This means your model will reference the location where it will actually be positioned. You do not want your model to be located according to a local coordinate system that only applies to your project or your estate, and not to the real-world.

Industry Foundation Classes (IFC) reference the location of your project using *IfcSite*, it provides the longitude, latitude and elevation using the world geodetic system *WGS84* (which is the same system used by GPS).

So apart from identifying that the project models should be located according to real-world coordinates, you should also identify a single designer or supplier to initially locate the project. For this to happen you will often need an accurate survey of the site, as the results of the survey may be modelled. The survey will also need to be located according to a real-world coordinate system.

Equipped with accurate survey information, a designer will be able to locate the project and provide your facility with real-world coordinates. The responsibility of providing this information will normally lie with the lead designer. The model coordinate information will be contained within the designer's model, and all other designers should use this information to their own models with real-world coordinates. This will make sure that when you combine (or federate) the individual IFC models, they will come together correctly. I still receive models where the coordinate information is incorrect, and results in the architectural and building services models appearing to be located in a different country.

12: A SCHEDULE OF ANY SOFTWARE FORMATS, INCLUDING VERSION NUMBERS, THAT SHALL BE USED BY THE SUPPLY CHAIN TO DELIVER THE PROJECT

This is another section where your particular needs dictate the amount of detail you include.

Most clients require no more than the project models in an IFC OpenBIM format, with the most common version being the *IFC 2x3* coordination view.

However, it is also advisable to ask your designers to also provide models in the format of the original authoring tool. When exporting to IFC from authoring software, some information will be removed. This information isn't required within the IFC model, but it may come in useful at a later date.

If you have a particular need to have your models in a proprietary format and version then this is where you should identify this requirement. For example, some Computer Aided Facility Management (CAFM) systems can communicate directly with Revit models through a Revit plugin.

> This is where you need to be fully aware of your organisational needs, the current systems that you use and any plans to implement new systems that may require specific formats.

It is always advisable to ask for open formats for your project models, unless you have a specific organisational need. This enables maximum engagement from your potential supply chain. All the popular model-authoring tools can export to IFC. And by specifying IFC you are not limiting your potential suppliers to those who use a particular authoring application. The IFC format will also ensure the long-term availability of your information and your models, as you are not depending on commercial software vendors to maintain support of a particular file type and version.

COMMERCIAL MANAGEMENT

1: EXCHANGE OF INFORMATION - ALIGNMENT OF INFORMATION EXCHANGES, WORK STAGES, PURPOSE AND REQUIRED FORMATS

This is where your EIR starts to get more interesting and more detailed.

This section clarifies what information is required, when it should be provided and in what format. This is where you start to detail exactly what you are using BIM for.

> *First, define the required project stages, ideally including completion dates.*

What system will you use for defining project stages? You should use an established system that is generally understood, if you want to avoid doing a whole section of work to define the requirements for each project stage.

The *RIBA Plan of Works*, the *CIC BIM Protocol* and *PAS 1192-2* all refer to a similar set of stages. The RIBA Plan of Works provides a very robust definition of each stage and a suite of documents that all help with managing project stages, as follows:

Stage 0 - Strategic Definition

Stage 1 - Preparation and Brief

Stage 2 - Concept Design

Stage 3 - Developed Design

Stage 4 - Technical Design

Stage 5 - Construction

Stage 6 - Handover and Close Out

Stage 7 - In Use

In this section, you should be clear about which system of stages that you will be following for your project. This will then enable you to define what information you will require, and how these releases of information, or data drops, align to the project stages. A data drop is the term used for the delivery of project information. However, through BIM Level 2 requirements, the UK government includes two data drops in Stage 2. It's also quite common to have two data drops during Stage 3 that, depending on the procurement route, align with the submission of planning and the completion of the stage.

Once you have detailed the number of data drops you need and when they should take place, you can identify the information you need to be fully informed at each data drop. The information you request should, during the design phase, enable you to make strategic and project decisions. For example, you may require information during the early stages of a project so you can objectively assess whether the project meets your business case. These are often seen as gateway questions: If the answers are not correct, a project should not proceed.

This section should remain relatively high-level, it should identify the types of information you need for each data drop, such as an IFC model, pdf drawing files or room data sheets in an a specific Excel file format.

How detailed the information should be and the responsibilities should be reserved for your model production and delivery table (MPDT). The detail of the data, the data format and the responsibilities should be contained within another file.

I often see this section completed with detailed information of why this data is required, and what decisions it will enable a client to make, but with no specifics of what information is needed in order for such decisions to be made. It assumes that the design team will know what information is required and will provide the relevant information. This is an odd approach, if you know what questions you need answering, you should know what information you need so those questions can be answered. Don't leave it to chance that you will be provided with the correct information. And if you don't know what information will be required so you can objectively answer your gateway questions, how can you expect your designers to know?

The final project data drop will consist of the handover of the completed, data-rich project models that represent your completed asset and will be used for managing your facility through its lifespan.

2: CLIENT'S STRATEGIC PURPOSES - DETAILS OF THE EXPECTED PURPOSES FOR INFORMATION PROVIDED IN MODELS

I find the literal requirements of this section, "strategic purpose" and "expected purposes", too vague to be really useful. Maybe it's useful to provide a narrative about your reason as a client to require a model with data? But I'm sure that it's even more useful to provide detail of actual purposes for a project model with data.

At BIMsense, we include employer purposes within all our EIRs. Employer purposes serve two roles. They provide a robust method of ensuring that, as a client, you have considered the most common purposes for requiring data within your model. It also means that you have made a conscious decision on the information that you do not want within the model. That is, the purposes you do not want to use the model for.

BS 1192-4 provides the most common employer purposes. We took a closer look at employer purposes in chapter 4.

Your EIR should list out all the employer purposes, identifying which will and will not be required.

It's also beneficial to expand upon the required employer purposes with details of the data sets that will provide the useable information.

For example, if you need the employer purposes for "management of capacity and utilization" then you could identify the IFC property set *Pset_SpaceOccupancyRequirements*, which has an *OccupancyNumber* attribute.

Such detail can be provided for each of the employer purposes and will provide an informative way of identifying the headlines of the data required within the model.

The detail of all the model data is still needed and will be provided elsewhere within your EIR.

3: A SCHEDULE OF ANY SOFTWARE FORMATS, INCLUDING VERSION NUMBERS, THAT SHALL BE USED BY THE SUPPLY CHAIN TO DELIVER THE PROJECT

This section is repeated from the Information Management section of requirements. My take on why the section is duplicated is that Information Management refers to the way information is managed throughout the project. Whereas in this section, Commercial Management, requirements cover specific project deliverables.

This means that the Information Management software formats refer to the software used for day-to-day design and BIM management, including the exchange of information for collaboration. And the Commercial Management software formats refer to those that will be used for delivering defined information, normally at the completion of stages.

I appreciate that this can be a cause for confusion. But this section shouldn't be too much of a problem to complete, as long as you have confirmed the formats of your information deliverables within your EIR.

It is important that you do provide this information. If you don't, you could be provided with the information in any format and it would be acceptable. There is a whole host of formats and ways that 3D models could be provided, included rarely used formats, such as 3D PDF.

The last time that we looked at software formats we focused on model formats and the importance of IFC, with IFC being the openBIM file format. You should also consider the other information you will receive and the associated file formats, the most common of which are below:

- Drawings - usually pdf, although you may want dwg or dwf, especially if you require an editable format.
- Documents - usually pdf, other options could include image files or Microsoft Word format.
- Schedules - if containing usable data, then use a spreadsheet (xlsx) format or possibly a csv, otherwise use pdf.
- COBie - the prescribed format from BS 1192-4 is Spreadsheet XML 2003 (which is an open spreadsheet format), you may want it in the more usual Microsoft Excel format or there is an alternative xml schema, which is known as COBie lite xml.

One final word on file formats. Navisworks software application forms part of the very successful Autodesk software suite, which includes Revit. Navisworks files can be exchanged with clash-detection information and, because of the wide popularity of Revit, Navisworks files are commonly exchanged between designers. The model checks from Navisworks are not as comprehensive as those that can be obtained from Solibri, as they don't use the advanced rule-based checks that are available within Solibri. However, Navisworks is a very useful application and, if used by your designers, you may also want to receive the Navisworks files.

4: AN INITIAL RESPONSIBILITY MATRIX SETTING OUT ANY DISCIPLINE RESPONSIBILITIES FOR MODEL OR INFORMATION PRODUCTION IN LINE WITH THE DEFINED PROJECT STAGES

The responsibility matrix is more commonly referred to as the model production and delivery table (MPDT). A typical example of an MPDT is provided within the CIC BIM Protocol (first edition). It provides a list of BIM deliverables, such as the architectural model and the building services model, and schedules these against the project stages and data drops. Then at each stage, or data drop, the responsible organisation is listed, along with the level of detail (LOD) required.

Before you go ahead and add the MPDT from the CIC BIM Protocol into your EIR there are a couple of things that you need to understand and consider.

LEVEL OF INFORMATION (LOI)

The MPDT was developed during the early days of BIM Level 2. It served a good purpose, providing a useful way of understanding responsibilities for BIM deliverables. And more importantly it brought level of detail (LOD) into the responsibility matrix. LOD is defined in another section of your EIR..

However, BIM processes have moved on since the MPDT was published. Most notably, in the use of level of information (LOI) in addition to LOD.

As LOD defines the graphical content of model entities, and LOI defines the data associated with model entities, it made sense to also include the LOI requirements within the MPDT. I'm sure you will be able to find many MPDTs with LOD and LOI that continue to be used on BIM projects.

This was how I produced MPDTs over the past couple of years.

But BIM processes have moved on yet again. What I am now doing is scheduling all data deliverables and responsibilities within a BIM data template, as it provides detail down to the individual attributes for each type of entity. This provides more detail than can be obtained through a LOI reference, which means there is no longer a reason to have LOI within the table. In fact by providing both a BIM data template and having an LOI within an MPDT you will bring in the potential for ambiguity.

MODEL DELIVERABLES

The typical MPDT within the CIC BIM Protocol provides an example list of models for delivery. These are the model types that are required to be delivered for each data drop. The list provided is a little confusing and not particularly helpful, it includes:

Overall form and content

Space planning

Site and context

Surveys

External form and appearance

Building and site sections

Internal layouts

Design strategies

Fire

Physical security

Disabled access

BREEAM

Performance

Building

4D Programming Analysis

Health and safety

Design

Construction

Operation

The list reads as more of a high-level responsibility matrix than a table that defines model production and delivery.

For example, an architectural design model would not have a separate model for space planning, it would be integral within the architectural model. And we couldn't look up what detail would be required within a space-planning model for LOD 3. The Uniclass LOD definitions are related to specific building entities or systems.

What you will normally find if looking at current iterations of an MPDT is a schedule of the different types of building elements - the actual components of a building - rather than types of design. The building elements are usually listed following either the NRM1 (New Rules of Measurement) codes or Uniclass 2015 codes.

These are then given a LOD and a responsibility for each data drop or project stage. If you use the BIM toolkit LOD definitions, this provides a relatively robust and simple way of identifying your requirements.

The main thing to be aware of if providing a fully scheduled MPDT is that you are essentially assigning definitive responsibilities for the design. This of course has upsides and downsides. The upside is that by assigning responsibilities you make it extremely clear exactly what you have appointed your designers to do. The downside is it is unlikely that the EIR will be the only document that identified each designer's scope of work. This means that you need to be sure that the information within the MPDT aligns with any other scope-of-work appointment documents.

If you wish, you can keep the MPDT really simple and break it down to generic model types, such as the architectural model, structural model and building services model. If you take this route you should still define the entities that should be included within your mode, elsewhere in your EIR.

5: A SCHEDULE OF THE STANDARDS AND GUIDANCE DOCUMENTS

Quite a simple one, this. It consists of a schedule of the current standards that should be followed in the delivery of your BIM project. It's almost a footnote to your EIR, as most of the UK BIM standards have been around for some time and are widely followed and accepted within the industry. The list of standards typically consists of:

> BS 1192:2007+A2:2016 *Collaborative production of architectural, engineering and construction information.* Code of practice to make the most of the collaborative working process, a common methodology for managing the data produced by and between all parties must be used. This should include the naming of data as well as a process for exchanging data.

> PAS 1192-2:2013 *Specification for information management for the capital/delivery phase of construction projects using Building Information Modelling.* This document provides information on the management of data produced within a BIM project environment, and supplements the processes and procedures contained in BS 1192:2007.

> PAS 1192-3:2014 (Corrigendum No. 1) *Specification for information management for the operational phase of assets using building information modelling.* This is a partner document to PAS 1192-2 focusing on the operational phase of assets for new and old buildings. Like PAS 1192-2, it applies to building and infrastructure assets.

> BS 1192-4:2014 *Collaborative production of information Part 4: Fulfilling employer's information exchange requirements using COBie.* This document defines expectations for the exchange of information for use throughout the lifecycle of a facility.

PAS 1192-5:2015 Specification for security minded building information modelling, digital built environments and smart asset management. This PAS outlines security threats to the use of information during asset conception, procurement, design, construction, operation and disposal. It addresses the steps required to create and cultivate an appropriate security mindset, and the security culture necessary for businesses to unlock new and more efficient processes and collaborative ways of working. The PAS has been developed to integrate a security-minded approach into the construction lifecycle processes as specified in PAS 1192-2 and the asset-management processes described in PAS 1192-3.

PAS 1192-6:2018 Specification for collaborative sharing and use of structured Health and Safety information using BIM. The PAS provides guidance on how health and safety information is produced, flows and can be used throughout the project and asset lifecycle. This PAS requires the contextualisation and filtering of hazards and risks to prioritise the elevated risks and aspects that are safety critical.

BS 7000-4:2013 Design management systems. Part 4. Guide to managing design in construction. This document provides guidance on management of the construction design process at all levels, for all organisations and for all types of construction projects. The guidance given applies to purpose-built constructions, equipment and components. It a key document for those who work in and with the construction industry, particularly designers and those managing design. Where general management principles are given, they may be adapted to suit any size of design organisation or construction project. The guidance applies to management of design activities throughout the life-cycle of a construction project, and the principles of the facilities management function.

BS 8536-1:2015 Briefing for design and construction. Code of practice for facilities management (Buildings infrastructure). BS 8536-1:2015 is part of the BIM Level 2 suite of documents that were developed to help the construction industry adopt BIM by 2016. It gives recommendations for briefing for design and construction, to ensure that designers consider the expected performance of a building in use. The standard applies to all new buildings projects and major refurbishments.

BS 8536-2:2016 Briefing for design and construction. Code of practice for asset management (Linear and geographical infrastructure). This is the only standard to provide briefing recommendations for the design and operational performance of infrastructure assets. It provides an evidence-based approach to design and construction, coordinating recommendations, not just from the asset-management standards (ISO 55000 series), but also the *BIM PAS's 1192-2, 1192-3 and 1192-5*, and Government Soft Landings.

Uniclass 2015 Classification, including LOD definitions, embedded within the NBS Toolkit. Uniclass2015 is a unified classification for the UK industry covering all construction sectors. It contains consistent tables classifying items of all scales, from a facility such as a library right down to products such as a CCTV camera within the library.

CIC/BIM Pro first edition 2013 Building Information Model (BIM) Protocol. The protocol identifies the BIMs that are required to be produced by members of the project team and puts into place specific obligations, liabilities and associated limitations on the use of the models.

It's unusual to move away from any of the above guidance documents. Although, if you want to move away from the NBS BIM toolkit definitions of LOD, it would make sense to identify the source of the project-specific definitions. Any bespoke requirements or alternative documents should be listed, while making sure they don't conflict with any of the above standards.

6: A SCHEDULE OF ANY CHANGES TO THE STANDARD COMPETENCES SET OUT IN THE CONTRACT

I'm not entirely sure that this should warrant its own section. It's more of a useful reminder. It's essentially saying that the information and the responsibilities within your EIR may conflict with information within other contract documents.

This is a very valid point. You may have added information within your EIR that goes above and beyond your requirements within some other document. However, a better and more robust approach would be to ensure that all your information aligns and remove any areas of ambiguity, rather than adding additional information that then attempts to clarify the differences.

COMPETENCE ASSESSMENT

1. DETAILS OF THE COMPETENCE ASSESSMENT THAT BIDDERS MUST RESPOND TO

This is where you should provide the detailed requirements of what you require from your bidders to enable you to assess their BIM competency.

You should refresh yourself with BIM competency in chapter 7, however, that main areas that you can use for assessing BIM competency are:

- BIM certification
- Standard assessment forms
- Experience
- Pre-contract BIM execution plan
- Example BIM model

2. CHANGES TO ASSOCIATED TENDER DOCUMENTATION

This section can be slightly confusing. However, to break it down, it's only referring to competence assessment. So, the way that I read this section, is that should the competence assessment requirements from the above *Details of the competence assessment that bidders must respond to* or the below *Changes to associated tender documentation* conflict or contradict other project competence assessments then this should be clearly detailed within this section.

So for example your project tender may identify that suppliers will be appointed with 60% of the overall scoring coming from quality assessments. This 60% score often includes items such as relevant project experience and an organisation's quality procedures. You may want to include the results of your BIM assessment within this overall quality score. Or alternatively BIM competency may be such an important requirement that if minimum level of BIM competency is required for a supplier to be considered.

Either way, your BIM requirements and any effect to your overall tender should be made clear. And ideally, all your documentation fully aligns, with BIM competency included within your project wide tender documentation, avoiding the need to include any information within this section.

3. BIM TENDER ASSESSMENT DETAILS

This is where you need to be clear on how you will assess the BIM competency evidence identified in the above section *Details of the competence assessment that bidders must respond to*. Which consists of the scoring that will be applied to the information, including any weightings that will be applied to the scores. And most importantly, whether there is any information, that has such a high importance, that suppliers will only be considered if they meet or exceed this level of competency.

It's always important to score tender returns using an objective approach and not, however tempting, to read between the lines. And finally you need to record the results of the assessment, which will enable you to explain, if ever required, the reasons for the scores.

CHAPTER SUMMARY

An EIR provides clear guidance on your BIM requirements for your project. It details exactly what the BIM deliverables will be, when they will be provided and who will provide them.

- An Employer's Information Requirement (EIR) is the number one important document to have in place for any BIM project.
- The three main areas within an EIR:
    - Information Management.
    - Commercial Management.
    - Competence Assessment.
- To make sure your EIR is as concise as possible, appraise your content. Does it:
    - Include enough information and detail for your requirements to be understood, and exclude information that is surplus to your requirements?
    - Include only information that is relevant and beneficial for the intended purpose?
    - Avoid ambiguous requirements?
- Without an EIR, it's very unlikely that you will receive the information that you require.

CHAPTER 12: ORGANISATIONAL AND ASSET INFORMATION REQUIREMENTS (OIR AND AIR)

Organisational Information Requirements (OIR) - *Data and information required to achieve the organisation's objectives.* (PAS 1192-3:2014)

Asset Information Requirements (AIR) - *Data and information requirements of the organisation in relation to the asset(s) it is responsible for.* (PAS 1192-3:2014)

Organisations managing large estates should have overarching Organisational Information Requirements (OIR) in place. From this, the specific detail of your Asset Information Requirements (AIR) can be generated. Then, for each BIM project, you produce a project-specific Employer's Information Requirements (EIR).

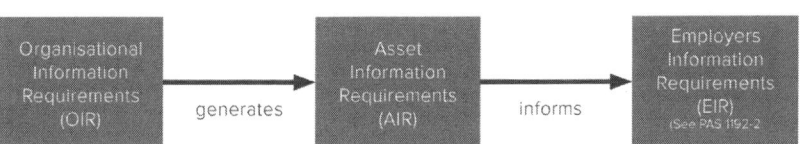

> Your OIR helps you to define the strategy behind your organisational data. It enables you to define what data you require across your whole organisation and the reasons for collecting this data.

It provides you with a quality assurance (QA) reference document, which acts as a baseline to allow you to compare the information you collect and use against what you have detailed that you require.

This allows valuable lessons to be learnt, and improvements made to your systems and processes. It's only by comparing your planned requirements against what actually happened that you will be able to either change your requirements or improve your systems.

Developing an OIR also provides a platform for integrating the whole of your organisational information requirements. This ensures that the information you obtain and manage is effective for all your departments and users. It can be too easy to just focus on obtaining data just for your own area of expertise. You will have a good understanding of what data will be useful to you and how you can use it. But applying this approach to other parts of your organisation will require the support of experts within each department.

ORGANISATIONAL INFORMATION REQUIREMENTS (OIR)

Organisation Information Requirements (OIR) is defined within *PAS 1192-3 Specification for information management for the operational phase of assets using building information modelling* as: "data and information required to achieve the organisation's objectives".

While *PAS 1192-3* does not fully define the content of an OIR - indeed within the document scope it states "This PAS does not cover data content as this is defined in the organizational information requirements (OIR) and asset information requirements (AIR)" - it does provide the typical content headings that could be found within an OIR:

- Optimising the asset management strategy and optimising/prioritising its asset management plan(s).
- Assessing the financial benefits of planned improvement activities.
- Modelling the asset to support operational decision-making.
- Determining the operational and financial impact of asset unavailability or failure
- Making life-cycle cost comparisons of alternative capital investments.
- Identifying expiry of warranty periods.

- Determining the end of an asset's economic life, for example, when the asset-related expenditure exceeds the associated income.
- Determining the cost of specific activities (activity-based costing), for example, the total cost of maintaining a specific asset(s)/asset system.
- Obtaining/calculating asset-replacement values.
- Undertaking financial analysis of planned income and expenditure.
- Obtaining/calculating the financial and resource impact of deviating from plans that might result in a change in asset availability or performance (for example, what is the financial impact of deferring the maintenance of a specific generator by six months?).
- Assessing its overall financial performance.
- Undertaking the ongoing identification, assessment and control of asset-related risks.

Your OIR should define all of your organisational information requirements and not just those that are obtained through a project model. Despite this, the development of a project model can help and simplify many of your organisational information requirements.

For example, warranty and life-cycle information can be added to individual assets in your project model, which will inform the ongoing costs of your estate.

It's notable that within the PAS 1192-3 OIR list, just one item explicitly refers to a model. That's not to say that your project model isn't a central part of obtaining OIR deliverables, it's just that you need to think beyond the immediate requirements of individual projects and take your OIR to a wider, whole-organisational level.

ASSET INFORMATION REQUIREMENTS (AIR)

Asset Information Requirements (AIR) is defined within *PAS 1192-3 Specification for information management for the operational phase of assets using building information modelling* as "data and information requirements of the organisation in relation to the asset(s) it is responsible for".

Your AIR provide the specifics of the data required for each asset. AIR are very similar to the BIM data template that we now provide within EIRs, which detail every data attribute that is required for every entity. Your AIR should go one step further - they should also detail asset data that is not contained within a project model. To give an example, this could be information that you use within your space-management software that provides the student numbers for your current courses. Your AIR should provide specific information on all such data.

DEVELOPING YOUR OIR AND AIR

Establishing your OIR and AIR from scratch will not be easy and it's a task that will never be complete. Your organisation's data needs and uses will continually evolve as your data maturity increases and new technology becomes available. You will also encounter some information requirements that just don't work, either because the data isn't currently available, or because it doesn't align fully with the intended use of the data.

For example, anticipated life information for assets is currently patchy. Some manufacturers will provide the information, while others do not or can not provide the data. If this information is required, you should continue to request it, but you need to understand the limitations and put measures in place to compensate for the gaps.

To fully establish your organisational data requirements you will need to involve all your departments. They will all have their own unique data needs and requirements. You will often need detailed discussions to fully understand the data needs of different departments, many of us are not used to thinking of our everyday activities in terms of their data uses.

You will have many different uses for facility and estates data within your different departments. Your space planning department will have detailed information on staff and student numbers, together with timetabling and space information. Your maintenance department will have information on equipment that requires regular replacement or servicing. And your strategic planning department will have information on anticipated future needs and the condition of the buildings within your estate.

Your data will never be perfect and at the start, you may find that much of the data you collect will not work for you or isn't available in the required format. But, as with everything, you need to start somewhere, and most things that provide long-term value take effort.

Taking the first steps to develop your OIR is very important. The first step will enable you to test your data and provide something visible that your organisation can provide objective feedback on.

Each project you undertake will enable you to refine your process and to obtain better, more relevant data. The longer you hold back on the first steps, the more difficult it will be to catch up with organisations that have already been through the most difficult part of the learning curve.

EVERYONE NEEDS TO BE INVOLVED

When establishing your OIR, all departments need to be involved. This isn't a task that can be delegated to one person. Of course, someone needs to take the lead and there need to be some clearly defined responsibilities. But, the input from your whole organisation is essential if you want to maximise the potential benefits. Otherwise, you may miss out on collecting data that could have massive value because no one explained what was required and why it was required.

It's not just a matter of blankly listing out a whole schedule of information required. Members of each department should look at what they currently do, and what information they use to undertake their tasks and perform their activities. Tasks and activities should be critically evaluated. For example, can they be done differently in a better way? Is there a piece of data that will enable them to do those tasks more efficiently? Or to do tasks that will provide more value?

CHAPTER SUMMARY

Your OIR helps you to define the strategy behind your organisational data. It enables you to define what data you require across your whole organisation and the reasons for collecting this data.

- An OIR provides you with a quality assurance (QA) reference document which acts as a baseline to allow you to compare the information you collect and use against the details of your requirements.
- Developing an OIR also provides a platform for integrating the whole of your organisational information requirements, not just those collected from a BIM project.
- Your AIR provides the specifics of the data required for each individual asset.
- When establishing your OIR, all departments need to be involved.

CHAPTER 13 - EMPLOYER'S DATA REQUIREMENTS AND BIM DATA TEMPLATE

BIM data template - *A template identifying the attributes (the data fields) required for each asset type, the template includes responsibilities and dates. (BIMsense)*

> *If you want data within your BIM model it's essential that you detail exactly what you want by providing a BIM data template.*

As an industry, since the UK Government established the BIM Level 2 timeline in 2011, we have made excellent progress in our use of BIM. But one area the design and construction industry still needs to improve upon is identifying the data we required within project models. Don't forget that BIM is providing us with new tools for managing project information in a more coordinated and joined-up approach. And the data within the model, within the data containers, is the method for organising our information.

The sections within Chapter 11: Employer's Information Requirements don't, in my opinion, give sufficient weight to the importance of defining your exact data requirements. Organisational Information Requirements (OIR) and Asset Information Requirements (AIR), as detailed in Chapter 12, provide better guidance for detailing data requirements.

But, before we get into the detail of the data template, let's look at a short history of why we are where we are with BIM.

THE MODEL AS A DESIGN TOOL (LATE 1990S TO 2010)

BIM primarily started as a 3D design tool. It made total sense to design what will be a 3D building in a 3D design application.

We then began realising the potential of using the model for its embedded data. Initially, this meant we extracted inherent information from a model. We could extract volumes and areas because the objects were detailed within the graphical model.

THE MODEL FOR COMPLEX DATA (2010 TO 2014)

This then moved into wanting the model to contain specification type information. We wanted manufacturer information about an asset or, as an example, the fire ratings of doors. The model started to be a container for our data, but a container without much structure. This was at the start of BIM Level 2, when we had lots of discussion around the possibilities of BIM but little in the way of actual deliverables.

At this point things began to get a little confused and disjointed. We had Revit - the most popular design authoring tool - which allowed predefined objects to be imported into the application. These predefined objects were often prepopulated with useful data. We had COBie (Construction Operations Building Information Exchange), which allowed embedded model information to be viewed in a spreadsheet format. COBie also became one of the BIM Level 2 deliverables. And we also had IFC (Industry Foundation Classes), developed by buildingSMART, which provided a comprehensive specification for an open format for building information models.

REQUESTS FOR MODEL DATA (2014 TO 2017)

This resulted in estate managers requesting data, reasonable requests such as wanting data to help with the management of assets during the lifetime of a building, or with space management. These data needs would be included within an EIR, but the requests themselves would be far too vague. Designers and contractors would have to establish what assets required managing, what information was required to enable the assets to be managed, what format was required and who was responsible for providing this information.

So, what we had at this stage, was the design and delivery team deciding what information should be provided, and what format it should be provided in.

Some clarity developed around data needs. Especially so for the management of assets, as these requirements linked closely with the data presented within COBie. Responsibilities were detailed for the delivery of information through complex responsibility matrices. And, as we looked at in the EIR chapter, the model product and delivery table (MPDT) from the CIC BIM Protocol (first edition) was adapted to include level of information (LOI). This identified responsibilities and provided an indication of how much information, and the type of information that should be provided.

Uniclass 2015 also provided assistance, enabling employers to schedule the assets that required data. Its System (Ss) and Product (Pr) tables provided a comprehensive list of building systems and components, from which critical and maintainable assets can be identified in a common and understandable format.

OUR DATA REQUIREMENTS NEED MORE DETAIL (2018)

This takes us to the current situation. We have EIRs that provide a significant amount of information through tables and schedules, detailing: the type of assets that require data; the type of data required; and the responsibilities for providing the data. But, we are still missing the specifics of exactly what data is required for each type of asset.

This may appear trivial, you may think that if all these requirements have been detailed then it can't be that difficult to provide relevant information. But that is missing the point, we are still requesting information, but not detailing exactly how we want it.

The current request for information is equivalent to applying for a passport without an application form. You would know that you need to provide relevant information about yourself. You could send HM Passport Office a letter or an email with the information. You would use your prior knowledge of what is required to include relevant information. But, the chances are that you may miss something relevant or provide something in the wrong format. And that would be just your application - each person who applied for a passport would send in something slightly different. Each application would have to be sorted, interpreted and assessed. This would be a wholly inefficient way of working. It would be far easier to detail exactly what is required and in what format.

Of course, that's not how we apply for a passport. We have an application form that details the exact information and the format of the information required for each application. This ensures that all required information is provided and the application is easily validated.

We now need the equivalent of a passport application form for BIM data. This would be in the form of a data template. A template detailing exactly the data required for each type of building asset. This BIM data template would form the centerpiece of employer's data requirements.

THE BIM DATA TEMPLATE

A BIM data template needs to clearly and unambiguously reference asset types. For each asset type, it needs to list the data attributes (the data fields), it needs to establish responsibilities for providing the data to populate those attributes and, finally, it needs to identify when the information is required.

The BIMsense data template has been released on GitHub. GitHub is a repository for storing information, but most importantly it provides versioning control to allow anyone to contribute to the development of the information.

ASSET TYPES

Asset types can be scheduled using the Uniclass 2015 System and Product codes. As we looked at in detail in the Chapter 8: Classifications, the use of classifications is essential for obtaining structured data within our model data containers.

Where possible, System (Ss) and Product (Pr) codes are provided within your data template for each asset that requires data. Although, your model should be fully classified, by your designers, with all assets and spaces, including those that don't require specific data.

Examples of assets that require specific data:

1. Cladding and lining panels (lightweight cladding and roofing panels) - *Pr_25_71_14; Wall cladding systems - Ss_25_20*
2. Fire doorsets - *Pr_30_59_24_28;* Door, shutter and hatch systems - *Ss_25_30_20*
3. Security shutters - *Pr_30_59_57_76*; Security systems - *Ss_75_40*
4. Buffer vessels - *Pr_60_50_20_10*; Hot and cold water supply systems - *Ss_55_70_38*

5. Water treatment dosing pots - *Pr_60_55_97_97*; Heating systems - *Ss_60_40_37*

6. Calorifiers and plate heat exchangers - *Pr_60_60_38*; Heating systems - *Ss_60_40_37*

7. Pressurisation units - *Pr_65_53_86_68*; Hot and cold water supply systems - *Ss_55_70_38*

8. Pressurisation units - *Pr_65_53_86_68*; Heating systems - *Ss_60_40_37*

9. Underfloor heating and cooling manifolds - *Pr_65_54_95_92*; Heating systems - *Ss_60_40_37*

10. Dirt separators - *Pr_65_55_76_22*; Heating systems - *Ss_60_40_37*

11. Demountable suspended ceiling systems - *Ss_30_25_22*

12. Floor covering and finishing systems - *Ss_30_42*

Each of the above 12 examples references specific assets, or types of assets for which data is required. Items 1-10 provide the detail of the system in which the asset will be located, plus the type of asset. Items 11 and 12 provide a generic requirement. This means that the same type of data is required for all demountable suspended ceiling systems, or for all floor covering and finishing systems, irrespective of the specific type.

It's also worth recapping on a couple of the items covered in Chapter 8: Classifications. The relationships between System (Ss) and Product (Pr) codes are not provided within Uniclass 2015. You will need to establish these yourself, or enlist the help of a BIM consultant to help you. It can appear daunting, but you just need to be clear on the assets for which you require data, the reasons why you want data (your employer purposes) and then methodically work through the tables to apply suitable codes.

The links between the System (Ss) and Product (Pr) tables have a many-to-many relationship. For example, in the above list, Heating systems - *Ss_60_40_37* occurs within items 5, 6 and 8, as three different types of products. And the asset Pressurisation units - *Pr_65_53_86_68* occurs within items 7 and 8, linked to two different types of systems. This means that a system will contain many types of products (or assets) and a product can be located within many different types of systems.

DATA ATTRIBUTES

This is where we provide the specific items of data, or data attributes, that are required for each asset or type of asset selected. However, before we get on to selecting the required data attributes, we need to have a basic understanding of the way data is arranged within a model.

It's massively useful to request our data requirements according to an existing framework and the information below applies specifically to IFC. As previously looked at, IFC is an open BIM format developed by BuildingSmart and is the preferred format for interoperability.

In this framework all assets and indeed any type of object (a building, a floor, a space and many other types) are generically grouped together as entities. All entities are grouped together in some way and usually have a project listed as the highest level of all the groups - the entity from which all other entities are linked. This is similar to the way that I describe a model as consisting of various data containers.

All entities within IFC have an *Ifc* prefix. For a project, the IFC entity is *IfcProject*, for a door we have IfcDoor. All IFC entities use CamelCase, this is where words (or in this case an acronym and a word) are joined together and the first letter of each is given a capital letter.

BuildingSmart provides a full listing of all the different types of IFC entities, with separate listings for IFC 2x3 and IFC4. IFC 2x3 and IFC4 are both different versions of IFC. IFC 2x3 is the most widely used version and has the best compatibility with software applications. IFC4 is the latest version, it has some benefits over IFC 2x3 including additional data types, but you should check for compatibility with your software before adopting IFC4. For clarity the details below refer to the IFC4.

Some entities have their own specific data attributes. For example *IfcDoor* has *OverallHeight* and *OverallWidth*, notice the use of *CamelCase* for the data attributes. The type of data that can be accepted within the attribute is also detailed, for *OverallHeight* and *OverallWidth* it's a positive number, or in other words a dimension, so this could be 2110 for the height and 910 for the width, with both measured in millimetres and referenced as *IfcPositiveLengthMeasure*.

However, individual object entities do not have that much attribute data. Property sets provide the bulk of data for objects. IFC has a whole set of predefined property sets, all linked to specific types of entities. Within each property set, there is a group of related attributes.

For an *IfcDoor*, we have a defined property set *Pset_DoorCommon*, which contains 16 different attributes such as *FireRating* and *AcousticRating* (once again all using *CamelCase*).

SO WHAT DOES ALL THAT MEAN FOR OUR DATA TEMPLATE?

You should currently have a list of assets for which we require data. These assets have been identified through their corresponding Uniclass 2015 codes.

You should now know what type of data you require and the purpose for obtaining the data, having established your employer purposes.

The next step is to select the IFC entity that aligns with each asset that needs data. For doors, this would be an IfcDoor. Next, select from the predefined IFC attributes and associated IFC property set attributes exactly which data is required to allow you to meet your employer purposes.

As an example, for *IfcDoor*, you may require the *support for compliance and regulatory responsibility* employer purpose. Data to enable you to meet this purpose should include information on fire compartments. So, any doors within a compartment wall will have a fire rating and each door should be regularly inspected to make sure it is able to perform correctly in the event of a fire.

Therefore, each relevant door - as identified through the Uniclass 2015 codes - has its own object, or entity, within your model. This will be type *IfcDoor*.

Don't forget that it's mandatory for assets such as doors to be registered for employer purposes. This will add Name (a unique door reference) and Description attributes to your asset, *IfcDoor*.

Manufacturer and warranty information is provided through attributes in the property sets *Pset_ManufacturerTypeInformation* and *Pset_Warranty*. The door fire rating is provided through the *FireRating* attribute with property set *Pset_DoorCommon*.

IFC Entity	IFC Property Set	IFC Attribute
IfcDoor	Pset_ManufacturerTypeInformation:	InformationManufacturer
IfcDoor	Pset_ManufacturerTypeInformation:	InformationModelReference
IfcDoor	Pset_ServiceLife:	ServiceLifeDuration
IfcDoor	Pset_Warranty:	WarrantyStartDate
IfcDoor	Pset_Warranty:	WarrantyEndDate
IfcDoor	Pset_Warranty:	WarrantyPeriod
IfcDoor	Pset_Warranty:	PointOfContact
IfcDoor	Pset_Warranty:	WarrantyContent
IfcDoor	Pset_Warranty:	Exclusions
IfcDoor	Pset_DoorCommon:	FireRating
IfcDoor	Pset_DoorCommon:	SmokeStop

Each predefined IFC attribute also has a predefined data type:

IFC Attribute	Data Type
InformationManufacturer	IfcLabel
InformationModelReference	IfcLabel
ServiceLifeDuration	IfcDuration
WarrantyStartDate	IfcDate
WarrantyEndDate	IfcDate
WarrantyPeriod	IfcTimeMeasure
PointOfContact	IfcOrganization
WarrantyContent	IfcText
Exclusions	IfcText
FireRating	IfcLabel
SmokeStop	IfcBoolean

As I'm sure you can begin to imagine, the amount of information within the data template starts to increase rapidly. It's essential that you detail exactly what is required and don't leave anything to chance. So, work through your assets and schedule the data that is required.

IFC provides a very comprehensive list of attributes. You can add your own property sets if the information you require to meet your employer purposes is not available within the available IFC attributes. The only minor restriction here is that your organisational bespoke property sets should not have the Pset_ prefix. The Pset_ prefix is reserved for the predefined IFC property sets. It is, however, a good idea to give a common prefix to any bespoke property sets, which will make them easy to identify.

RISK PROPERTY SETS

You may recall from reading about employer purposes , within Chapter 4: Establishing your organisational data requirements, support for compliance and regulatory responsibilities, involved collecting health and safety and risk information.

I mentioned that there is a property set for risk. However, going forward, we may have two risk property sets available to us: the *IFC Pset_Risk* property set and the *PAS 1192-6 HS_Risk_UK* expanded risk property set.

To give you a flavour of the information that is grouped within IFC-defined *Pset_Risk*, it includes:

- Risk Type (*RiskType*) – a predefined list of risk types, such as HAZARD, HEALTHANDSAFETY, INSURANCE and OTHER.

- Nature of Risk (*NatureOfRisk*) and Sub Nature of Risk (*SubNatureOfRisk1 & 2*) – a method of describing the risk in increasing detail.

- Assessment of Risk (*AssessmentOfRisk*) – a means for categorising the likelihood of occurrence using a predefined list, such as ALMOST CERTAIN, VERY LIKELY, LIKELY, VERY POSSIBLE, POSSIBLE, SOMEWHAT POSSIBLE, UNLIKELY and VERY UNLIKELY.

- Risk Consequence (*RiskConsequence*) – an indication of the severity of the outcome should the risk occur and provides a predefined list, such as CATASTROPHIC, SEVERE, MAJOR, CONSIDERABLE, MODERATE, SOME, MINOR, VERY LOW and INSIGNIFICANT.

- Risk Rating (*RiskRating*) – This provides the general rating of the risk and a predefined list, such as CRITICAL, VERY HIGH, HIGH, CONSIDERABLE, MODERATE, SOME, LOW, VERY LOW and INSIGNIFICANT.

- Risk Owner (*RiskOwner*) – This determines who owns the risk and provides a predefined list, such as DESIGNER, SPECIFIER, CONSTRUCTOR, INSTALLER, MAINTAINER and OTHER.

The risk property set enables you to collate all significant risks and hazards within a model. The IFC risk property sets (*IFC Pset_Risk*) can be linked to physical objects, processes or activities.

WHEN THE INFORMATION IS REQUIRED

I have jumped over the issue of responsibilities for the time being. This is because instead of providing a responsibility matrix similar to the Model Product and Delivery Table, responsibilities can be simplified. However, to understand the simplification, it's useful to consider firstly when the information is required.

There are two steps to providing the required data:

- Provide a template of the data within the model (this is different from the data requirements template). This means that all the data attributes for a given asset type are contained within your model. Many, if not all, of these attributes will not contain any data when first added to the model. They will initially appear as blank data fields for each required attribute.

- Provide the correct specific data for each of the blank attribute fields.

The best and most rational approach is to have the full blank attribute set applied to each asset type as soon as it is added to a model. This means that as soon as doors, for example, are added to a project model (usually at RIBA stage 2), all the blank attribute fields that will require data at some point during the project are all added to each door.

This is an efficient way of working, designers can develop object templates with all the required data fields ready to be dropped into models. It also allows the data within the project model to be validated against the requirements of the data requirements template.

This means that for each required attribute in the data template, there will be two dates. The first will identify when the individual asset object type (and subsequently the blank attribute) should be added to the project model (see step 1, above). The second date will identify when the actual data should be added to the blank attribute (see step 2, above). Sometimes, the date for the attribute template will be the same as the actual data, information such as Names and Descriptions will be added as soon as the asset is included within the model.

RESPONSIBILITIES FOR PROVIDING THE DATA

This then leads us on to responsibilities for providing the data. When it comes to providing the information, both the procurement route for the project and when the construction and delivery team is appointed will have an effect on responsibilities for the information.

It's also important that when you identify a responsible organisation, you are consistent in identifying the ultimate responsibility and not a delegated responsibility.

At the early stages of a project, usually at RIBA stages 2 and 3, your main designers, architect, structural engineer and building services engineer will be responsible for providing your data. For design-and-build projects, where a contractor takes on the responsibility for design as well as construction, the contractor will also take on the responsibility for providing data at either stage 4 or stage 5. With traditional contracts, in which designers remain responsible for design and a contractor only has responsibility for the construction of a building, the responsibility for data is a little more complicated and we will unpick this later.

Let us first consider a design-and-build procurement route where a contractor is appointed at stage 4. You will have a design team developing information through to stage 3 and then from stage 4, the contractor will be responsible for completing the design, followed by construction and handover. In the last section of this chapter, I identified two dates for providing information for each and every item of data. The first of these provides the data template (or the blank data field) and the second provides the relevant piece of data, the information required to populate the data field.

Because you have identified the specific items of required data for each type of asset (the assets are identified through our Uniclass 2015 codes), you are able to assign the asset types to a design discipline. By going down to the granular level of a specific door type of a fire damper within a ventilation duct, you will be able to clearly identify the responsible designer. When an asset type is assigned with a responsibility, the individual required items of data for an asset type will also follow the same responsibility.

So if you require data for Fire doorsets - *Pr_30_59_24_28* then the designer responsible for including fire doors within a project model would be the architect. It follows that the architect would be identified as the responsible designer for providing all the associated data - both the data template and the populated data. This clearly works for the data template and for some, but not all, of the data required to populate the data fields. However, you have already identified that for a design-and-build project, the contractor becomes responsible for the completing the design and delivering the finished building. So, if an item of populated data has a required date at stage 5 and a contractor is appointed at stage 4, the responsibility for providing the data transfers to the contractor. It then becomes the responsibility of the contractor to obtain the data and ensure that the information is added to the model.

This means you can keep your data requirements template as simple as possible. I know that the template contains lots of information, and in itself is not simple, but you shouldn't add unnecessary information. You have managed to avoid listing out every project stage and identifying a responsible organisation at each stage. Instead, identify the responsible design discipline and the stages that require the blank data field and the populated data.

Design Discipline	Date Template	Populated Data
1. Architectural	Stage 3	Stage 3
2. Architectural	Stage 3	Stage 5
3. MEP	Stage 3	Stage 3
4. MEP	Stage 3	Stage 5

Each of the above items represents an individual item of data. Let's assume it's for a design-and-build project, where the contractor is appointed after the completion of stage 4.

The data templates within the model are required at stage 3 for all the items. The first two items are assigned to the architectural discipline and the second two items to the building services design discipline Mechanical, Electrical and Plumbing (MEP).

The populated data for items 1 and 3 is required at the same time as the model data template, this could be the name of the objects.

The populated data for items 2 and 4 are not required until stage 5. For a design-and-build project the contractor would be appointed and would assume responsibility for providing the information, this could be the installation date for the items. The contractor would most likely delegate these responsibilities to designers or sub-contractors.

Traditional projects are a little more complicated when establishing responsibilities, as the design responsibility remains with the individual design organisations. Although, what actually happens is that a contractor assumes design responsibility for some elements of a project, such as cladding or roof finishes. For this type of project, the designers are responsible for providing the final-issue (or as-built) design information. This is information that correctly aligns with the actual construction of a building. It's common for the constructed facility to differ slightly from the design. The design information then needs to be updated to include these changes.

Therefore, the responsibility for providing the model with the required data will remain with the individual designers throughout the project. However, once the contractor has been appointed, the contractor will be responsible for providing the required data to the responsible designer. Looking back at the previous example:

Design Discipline	Date Template	Populated Data
1. Architectural	Stage 3	Stage 3
2. Architectural	Stage 3	Stage 5
3. MEP	Stage 3	Stage 3
4. MEP	Stage 3	Stage 5

For item 2 the contractor will provide the individual item of data to the architect who will add the information to the architectural model. Similarly for item 4, the data will be provided to the building services designer for inclusion with the building services model.

In addition, should the data for item 1 change during the construction of the facility, the contractor will also be required to ensure that the correct information has been provided to the architect, who will then be able to update the architectural model.

This provides a relatively simple and clear approach to objectively defining responsibilities.

THE COMPLETED DATA REQUIREMENTS TEMPLATE

Now it's over to you to develop your data requirements template. Here's a step-by-step guide:

- Establish your organisation data requirements through the employer purposes.
- Select the asset types for which data will be required.
- Assign Uniclass 2015 classification codes to each of the asset types.
- List the specific data (or attributes) that will be required for each asset type.
- Assign the design discipline responsible for the asset types.
- Schedule and assign when the model data template is required for each asset type.
- And, finally, assign when the populated data is required for each individual item of data

A fully developed data requirements template will enable you to identify exactly what you want. And just as importantly, you will have the means to objectively assess the progress of your designers and contractor in providing your data. You can look at the design discipline models at any stage and assess whether the data has been provided in line with your data requirements template.

I'm sure that you will agree that this process is a massive improvement on the existing ad-hoc approach that we currently take when obtaining as-built information. It should also assist all those responsible for providing information - organisations prefer to know exactly what is required from them, as it enables them to plan and manage their workflows.

CHAPTER SUMMARY

If you want data within your BIM model it's essential that you detail exactly what you want by providing a BIM data template.

- A BIM data template needs to clearly and unambiguously reference asset types. For each asset type, it needs to list the data attributes (the data fields), it needs to establish responsibilities for providing the data to populate those attributes and, finally, it needs to identify when the information is required.

- BIMsense has released the BIM data template on GitHub, however, if you want to start from scratch:

    - Establish your organisation data requirements through the employer purposes.
    - Select the asset types for which data will be required.
    - Assign Uniclass 2015 classification codes to each of the asset types.
    - List the specific data (or attributes) that will be required for each asset type.
    - Assign the design discipline responsible for the asset types.
    - Schedule and assign when the model data template is required for each asset type.
    - And, finally, assign when the populated data is required for each individual item of data

- A fully developed data requirements template will mean you will be able to identify exactly what you want. And just as importantly, you will have the means to objectively assess the progress of your designers and contractor in providing your data.

CHAPTER 14: FINAL COMMENTS

BIM is a very wide-reaching subject, it affects every aspect of design, construction and the management of a facility. This book is narrowly focused on how BIM can benefit an organisational estate and the methods for obtaining the information that will facilitate the benefits. As such, BIM for construction management is beyond the scope of this book and we have also not looked at some of the amazing virtual and augmented reality uses of detailed project models.

COLLABORATION

> Collaboration is the glue that binds us all into this new way of working. Collaboration is absolutely essential to all successful BIM projects.

Every step identified within this book should involve collaboration, either between teams within your organisation, or with your design and construction suppliers during the delivery of a new project.

The foundations to effective collaboration during the delivery of a project is having clear and unambiguous information. Information that defines exactly what you require and when you require it from your team.

This can only be provided through a comprehensive and well developed EIR and, of course, if you need professional assistance with this, then BIMsense would be happy to help.

BENEFITS OF BIM

Throughout this book I have identified the direct benefits that you and your organisation will obtain from BIM, such as the easy access to information about your facility throughout the design and during the use of your building.

Efficiencies during the design stages make it more likely that you will get the facility that meets your organisational needs and reduce the risk of costly and time-consuming design changes.

There are the benefits of delivering a safe building, in which hazards are identified and eliminated. And the way these benefits continue throughout the life of your facility, enabling you to simply access, assess and manage your maintenance activities.

These long-term benefits increase the return on your BIM investment.

I'm convinced that these benefits will turn out to be just the tip of the iceberg. When the internet (or, more accurately, the world wide web) came into existence in 1989, nobody could have predicted the effects that are continuing to be felt, such as social media, the smartphone and many aspects of collaborative BIM.

BIM will continue to evolve, its reach will widen and we discover innovative beneficial uses of the data models.

TECHNOLOGICAL EVOLUTION

Anecdotally, it appears that technology is evolving at an ever-increasing rate. This can be seen as concerning and problematic, introducing questions such as how can I ever keep up with the technological changes?

It's clear to me that if you continue doing things the same way as you have always done, then it will not be possible to keep up with, and benefit from, technological changes.

You need to experiment and introduce a whole suite of tools, with BIM being one of those tools, to enable you to move and adapt in an agile way.

As an example of the speed of technological change, since I began writing this book at BIMsense, we have seen the following:

- We have tools for directly adding classifications to IFC models, which have been developed directly because of the importance of classifications as discussed in Chapter 8.

- We have tools for directly adding the BIM data template to IFC models.

- We are using GitHub for sharing and improving our information, initially with the community release of our BIM data template

- We have launched a new web tool for managing projects using an EIR, this will evolve to include a whole set of additional services such as the above classification and data template tools.

One useful tool for keeping up with the advances in technology is to gather information from trustworthy sources, if you want to be kept informed of the latest developments at BIMsense please sign-up to our newsletter.

YOUR BIM JOURNEY

The first steps into anything new are always the most difficult ones: you will have the fear of the unknown. Hopefully, this book has helped to reduce those fears, eliminate some of the unknowns and has directed you along a path without requiring too many U-turns.

As you continue along your BIM journey, you will increase your knowledge and develop your own individual approaches. There isn't a single correct way of "doing" BIM. It's evolving and will continue to evolve. We will develop better and more efficient ways of developing, delivering and using our information models. Remember:

- You should maintain a critical mind, don't blindly accept statements without understanding the evidence.

- Try to keep everything as simple as possible. BIM can appear complicated, so don't add unnecessary requirements. Only request the information that you require and keep your requirements unambiguous and clear. If you are finding it hard to describe your requirements, then it's often a sign that you don't fully understand something, or you don't really know what you require.

- This book focuses on the data within your models. Your data should be structured and ordered, this allows objective validation of the data and reliable and accurate assessments.

- And finally, continue to learn and share your knowledge. Learn from your mistakes, don't worry, we have all made them. Improve your processes. The cumulative benefits will become evident and will benefit your organisation. Learn more about the data within the model and the possible ways that you can use that data. Then take this knowledge and share it with others within your organisation, but also share it with those outside of your organisation. We all need to improve, and find new and better ways of using the available technology. If we all move forward together, we will increase the rate of innovation from which we will all benefit.

I wish you all the best in your BIM journey, I hope it's successful and that it provides you and your organisation with the benefits that are available. And I hope that, in turn, we all make a small contribution to improving construction.

If you require any help feel free to contact me at ian.yeo@bimsense.co.uk and I would also welcome any feedback that could help to improve the content of this book for others.

And one last thing, if you have in anyway found this book helpful, please help others to discover this book by leaving a review on Amazon.

CHAPTER 15 - GLOSSARY OF TERMS

AIR - Asset Information Requirements, data and information requirements of the organisation in relation to the asset(s) it is responsible for. (PAS 1192-3:2014)

API - Application Programming Interface, a set of functions and procedures that allows the creation of applications which access the features or data of an operating system, application, or other service.

Autodesk's Revit - One of many design-authoring applications for use in BIM projects

BCF - BIM Collaboration Format, a file format that allows issues to be collected together and managed in a collaborative and efficient way.

BIM - Building Information Modelling, a process for creating and managing information throughout the lifecycle of a project.

BIM Execution Plan - A supplier's response to an EIR, confirming that supplier's interpretation of the EIR and how it proposes to deliver a client's BIM requirements.

BIM Level 2 - A level of BIM maturity. In the UK, a suite of standards and guidance documents define the requirements of BIM Level 2.

BIM levels - A way of defining BIM maturity, from BIM level 0 (a project without BIM) through to BIM level 3 (which has yet to be fully defined, but consists of four intermediate levels 3A, 3B, 3C and 3D).

BIM wash - where a BIM competency claim is greater than the actual BIM competency of a person or organisation.

BRE - Building Research Establishment, a leading centre of building- and construction-related scientific research.

BRE Green Guide to Specification - Environmental guidance for selecting construction materials and products.

BREEAM - Building Research Establishment Environmental Assessment Method, a method for assessing the impact of a construction project.

BS 1192:2007+A2:2016 - Collaborative production of architectural, engineering and construction information. A code of practice to make the most of the collaborative working process.

BS 1192-4:2014 - Collaborative production of information Part 4: Fulfilling employer's information exchange requirements using COBie. This document defines expectations for the exchange of information for use throughout the lifecycle of a facility.

BS - British Standard, a code of practice providing robust guidance and processes.

BuildingSMART - an industry-backed, not-for-profit community developing open standards.

CAFM - Computer Aided Facilities Management, software applications for managing facilities.

CAPEX - Capital expenditure to acquire, upgrade and maintain physical assets.

CAWS - Common Arrangement of Work Sections, a 1987 method of classification.

CDM regulations - Construction (Design & Management) Regulations 2015, regulations for managing health, safety and welfare on construction projects.

CIC BIM Protocol - A supplementary legal agreement that identifies the models that are required to be produced by members of the project team, and puts into place specific obligations, liabilities and associated limitations on the use of the models.

Classifications - Classification is a method of putting something into a group or category. Common construction classification systems include Uniclass 2015 and Omniclass.

COBie - Construction Operations and Building Information Exchange, a method for exchanging information in a structured format.

Data drops - A delivery of defined project information, data drops often align with project stages such as those provided by the RIBA Plan of Works.

Dumb data - Data that doesn't link or directly relate to other data.

EIR - Employer's Information Requirements. A pre-tender document that sets out the information to be delivered, and the standards and processes to be adopted by the supplier as part of the project delivery process. (PAS 1192-2:2013)

Employer's data requirements - The specific data requirements of an employer, avoiding generic or ambiguous terms.

GUID - Globally Unique Identifier.

IFC - Industry Foundation Classes, a platform-neutral and open specification for construction data.

Information Manager, Organisational - Responsible for an organisation's building models and information after the completion of a project.

Information Manager, Project - Ensures that project BIM procedures as defined within an EIR and a supplier's BEP are followed and that information provided satisfies the BIM deliverables.

ISO - International Organization for Standardization.

Live loads - Live loads, or imposed loads are temporary loads such as those from the occupants of a building.

LOD - Level of detail, describes the detail or the complexity of the graphical contents of a model.

LOI - Level of information, describes the detail or the complexity of the data (non-graphical) contents of a model.

LOMD - Levels of Model Definition, the combination of both graphical (LOD) and non-graphical information (LOI)

Many-to-many relationships - When one or more items in one table has a relationship to one or more items in another table.

Mapping, data - A method of linking similar items of data from different sources.

Model checking - Verifying the accuracy and quality of building information models.

NBS - An organisation that develops building specifications and the custodians of Uniclass 2015.

NBS BIM toolkit - A BIM project management tool that includes Uniclass 2015 LOD definitions.

New Rules of Measurement (NRM) codes - NRM is a comprehensive set of measurement rules and cost management guidance with codes provided for the elemental breakdown.

OIR - Organisational Information Requirements - Data and information required to achieve the organisation's objectives. (PAS 1192-3:2014)

openBIM - An open approach to collaboration through sharing building information by buildingSMART.

OPEX - Operating expense, the in-use ongoing cost of a running a facility.

Organisational project manager - The person assigned with the responsibility of delivering capital investment projects, such as a new or refurbished facility.

PAS 1192-2:2013 - Specification for information management for the capital/delivery phase of construction projects using Building Information Modelling.

PAS 1192-3:2014 (Corrigendum No. 1) - Specification for information management for the operational phase of assets using building information modelling.

PAS 1192-5:2015 - Specification for security-minded building information modelling, digital built environments and smart asset management.

PAS 1192-6:2018 - Specification for collaborative sharing and use of structured health and safety information using BIM.

PAS documents - A Publicly Available Specification is a document that responds to a rapidly developing industry need and is produced to provide immediate structure and guidance. A PAS is normally replaced by a BS within two years.

Planned Preventative Maintenance (PPM) - Maintenance that is planned and scheduled for the purpose of maximising the life of assets.

Point cloud survey - Laser scanning to create a cloud of geometrically located points.

Quality assurance - A management process to maintain the quality of a product or service.

RIBA - Royal Institute of British Architects.

RIBA Plan of Works - A method of defining the design and delivery stages of a construction project.

Uniclass 2015 - A unified classification for the UK industry covering all construction sectors.

First Edition. March 2018

Copyright © Ian Yeo (2018). All rights reserved.

Publisher: BIMsense Limited
www.bimsense.co.uk

For any inquiries regarding this book, please email:
ian.yeo@bimsense.co.uk

No part of this book may be reproduced in any form or by any electronic or mechanical means, including information storage and retrieval systems, without written permission from the author, except for the use of brief attributed quotations.

Editor: Jo Charlton
www.jocharlton.com

Cover design, images & formatting: Mattix Design
www.mattixdesign.com

Printed in Great Britain
by Amazon